A NIGHT AT THE DISCO

ALICE HARRIS AND CHRISTIAN JOHN WIKANE

ACC ART BOOKS

A Night at the Disco is a tribute to all of the artists and musicians who got us on the dance floor... and still keep us dancing.

— Alice Harris and Christian John Wikane

CONTENTS

FOREWORD

The true beginning of dance music and nightclubs was during the 1970s. The club scene was happening—*everything* was happening! Studio 54 was the big one. Most people were going to clubs till two o'clock in the morning, going to bed, then going to work at eight! That had a lot to do with the disc jockeys. You never knew what they were gonna pick next, but the music they were playing was so popular, it would eventually move to radio. ● The '70s sort of went into three periods. At the beginning there was the "message" music—Sly & the Family Stone and things like that. As it got to the middle, it got more song oriented. Barry White did a lot of great work. The songs got better and better. There was a lot of good stuff on the landscape. You also had *The Wiz*—the play that was on Broadway with Stephanie Mills—which we were influenced by. George Faison, our choreographer, had worked on *The Wiz*. We were influenced by Ashford & Simpson and Gamble & Huff. The record companies at the time all had R&B divisions and they were all pumping out records. I used to get free records from every label just to listen to the things that were coming out. All the labels were on fire. ● At the end of the '70s, it was all about the dance. The production and song quality on a lot of these records was fantastic, sonically. What Donna Summer did with Giorgio Moroder was really great—"toot toot, beep beep"! Those were some *really* good records that she did and her success was so huge. CHIC was the perfect disco band. They played those grooves, man. Michael Jackson was one person who was really paying attention and watching it. He was at Studio 54 like we were. He was able to take that music and put it all in *his* music. *Off the Wall* (1979) was a great record—musically, what Quincy Jones did was put Michael in a frame where he sounded really mature. ● We had great times. We were in the studio every day. We didn't think of it as "dance music," we just thought of it as *good* music. We knew that "Shining Star" was going to be a big hit. The hook, the chorus, the lyrics... I thought it was great. "September" is the gift that keeps on giving. I think it's one of those songs that *everybody* loves. A house band could play that song and get a standing ovation. It's been in movies and on television. The month of September is Earth, Wind & Fire's month! "Boogie Wonderland" was a great song to cut. We got a GRAMMY Award for *just* the track! ● The music of the '70s was real music. The chord changes, the strings sounded great, the horns sounded great. They're *songs*. It was exciting. It was music the way that music was supposed to be.

Verdine White
Earth, Wind & Fire

INTRODUCTION

Disco began with the discothèque. Before it was a musical style or a sensibility, disco was a place. A French term that translates to "record library," the discothèque, and its shortened sobriquet, became a destination for imagination and fantasy. It's where disc jockeys reigned supreme, spinning and mixing records to mesmerizing effect. ● "Discothèque music," or music that DJs played in the clubs, encompassed soul, funk, pop, rock, and percussive-driven styles from across the globe during the early '70s before a confluence of elements formed a definable genre of music. "There is a disco beat, but the music that went over it can be varied," says Melba Moore, who recorded with dance-music dynamos like Van McCoy, Pete Bellotte, and McFadden & Whitehead throughout the '70s. "The *music* moved you to want to get on the dance floor." ● Dancing was the ultimate form of self-expression—especially with fashion designed to accentuate the body under swirling lights—and discothèques galvanized the liberating power of the beat. As original CHIC vocalist Alfa Anderson said, "Disco was always a place where people could get away from society's restrictions... The world puts you in a box, but when you're on the floor dancing, and you grab somebody's hand, it doesn't matter whose hand it is. That's what disco gave to the world." ● *A Night at the Disco* celebrates the story of disco through the artists who made it happen. It reflects a progression of sounds and styles that evolved between 1970 and 1979, dance music's most seminal era: from orchestral masterpieces by Isaac Hayes and Barry White to groups like Silver Convention and Dr. Buzzard's Original Savannah Band, whose music introduced new textures to the clubs; plus, musical giants like James Brown and Sly & the Family Stone, who laid the foundation for the dance music revolution of the 1970s. *A Night at the Disco* also shows how pop artists like Cher and ABBA tailored their sound for the clubs and were rewarded with blockbuster hits or, where the Bee Gees were concerned, a GRAMMY Award-winning soundtrack. ● "It was a very interesting time to me," said Donna Summer, remembering her ascent as the Queen of Disco. "Everybody was on *fire*. They were on fire with the love of what they were doing and the hope of success. They were on fire with the knowledge that they were doing something that might last longer than just a few weeks. Everybody just poured themselves into what was going on." Musically, discothèques mirrored that combination of passion and boundless creativity. "People are always going to want to dance," says Valerie Simpson. "If they can get a melody and a thought, and something that is uplifting while they're moving, then it has a chance to last." Five decades later, the dance music of the 1970s retains its power to move and inspire. ● *A Night at the Disco*—you could see anything and anything could happen. Music was the force behind it all. The artists on these pages welcome you to the dance floor...

1970-1973

"1968 was the first time I heard about disco," recalls original Santa Esmeralda vocalist Leroy Gómez. "I was working with Tavares in Boston. In those days, the band would play and everybody would dance. Then when the disc jockey would get up, everybody would sit down and they would serve drinks. I was dating a Jamaican girl that was going to school in Switzerland. This girl told me, 'In Europe, there are no bands. The disc jockey plays the records and everybody dances to the records.' We all chuckled and said, 'Are you kidding me?'"

Discothèques were primed to flourish in the 1970s and it was New York City that became the nexus for a burgeoning cultural and musical phenomenon. In 1970, French impresario Olivier Coquelin opened Hippopotamus on East 54th St., expanding his empire of Manhattan nightclubs from the 1960s, comprising Le Club, Ondine, and Cheetah. *New York Magazine* quipped that Coquelin's latest conquest was "heir to the discothèque crown" of Arthur, a prime haunt for celebrities and the jet set that Sybil Burton ran from 1965-1969, and the Peppermint Lounge, which re-emerged in the '70s as a gay club called Hollywood, and then again as G.G.'s Barnum Room. Two blocks from the unmarked door of Hippopotamus, the fashionable Shepheard's at the Drake Hotel advertised a succinct definition of discothèques: "Dancing to records *plus.*"

Beginning in 1971, The Best of Friends (TBOF) social club produced weekly dance soirées at several Manhattan venues like the Ginza, La Martinique, Casablanca, Al Mounia, and Barney Google's before opening three of the first Black-owned clubs in midtown Manhattan: Leviticus, "the only place to be" according to WBLS FM; Othello; and Bogard's. TBOF's emergence also paralleled the national debut of *Soul Train* on television in October 1971. "When Black folks watched *Soul Train*, it wasn't just for the entertainment value of the show, it was to pick up new dance moves and to check out the fashions that people were wearing," wrote TBOF co-founder Noel Hankin in his 2021 book, *After Dark*. "Dressing up for a night club was an essential part of the fun."

Legendary fashion designer Stephen Burrows favored Sanctuary, a club west of midtown in Hell's Kitchen, which had opened in 1969 and became one of the first major gay discothèques in the US. "Heaven had come to earth," he says, recalling how innovative DJs like Francis Grasso and Steve D'Acquisto quenched dancers' insatiable desire, mixing James Brown, Sly & the Family Stone, The Rolling Stones, Led Zeppelin, and Nigerian drummer Olatunji into nights of unfettered abandon.

Gay liberation blossomed alongside the beat, from Fire Island clubs like the Sandpiper and Ice Palace to a proliferation of discos in Manhattan, including Haven, The Gallery, Better Days, Tenth Floor, and Continental Baths, where future DJ legends Larry Levan and Frankie Knuckles got their start. The Loft, however, held a special place. At the time, *New York Magazine* deemed it "the masterpiece of the New York discothèque: an unbeatable sound system, remarkable refreshments, and the most sophisticated and varied collection of hard partyers ever to cram a dance floor" (1974).

David Mancuso, owner and DJ, had begun hosting rent parties at his loft downtown on Broadway in 1968 before launching his first weekly dance party on Valentine's Day 1970—"Love Saves the Day" (L.S.D.). Though the Loft had an invitation-only policy to retain its intimate, communal vibe, the crowd spanned New York's cultural and socioeconomic spectrum. "I went through the '60s, with the whole psychedelic movement, civil rights," Mancuso later said in an interview with Red Bull Music Academy. "I had certain things I wanted to do to send a message. It had more to do with social progress, because you had mixed economic groups. You had people from all sorts of different backgrounds, cultures... Gay, straight, bi, Black. Everybody."

The advent of discothèques throughout Manhattan mirrored a groundswell of sonic experimentation in records that would ripple across the new decade. Sly Stone, Isaac Hayes, and Ashford & Simpson were among the songwriters and producers who'd already mastered the craft of making danceable, three-minute singles during the late '60s. No longer confined to the constraints of AM radio, they created expansive musical experiences well suited for DJs who were shaping sets for all night dancing.

"Sparked by East Coast discothèques, long songs with hypnotizing instrumental counter-rhythms have been scoring hit after hit," *Billboard* reported in 1973. "Among the best examples are the Temptations' 'Papa Was a Rolling Stone' and Manu Dibango's 'Soul Makossa.'" Indeed, as Motown Records grew more progressive with Marvin Gaye's *What's Going On* (1971) and Norman Whitfield's productions for The Temptations, "Soul Makossa" represented another facet of club music, with DJs combing through singles and albums by European-based acts like Osibisa, Barrabás, and Cymande, who combined West African rhythms with elements of funk, rock, and jazz. WBLS DJ Frankie Crocker, who regularly visited the Loft, helped break "Soul Makossa" on the airwaves where Dibango's original version became a Top 40 pop hit, even as nearly a dozen cover versions flooded the market.

While any song by James Brown was guaranteed to pack a dance floor, the records that Kenny Gamble and Leon Huff were producing for artists on Philadelphia International Records—MFSB, The O'Jays, Harold Melvin & the Blue Notes, The Intruders, The Three Degrees, among others—were distinguished by a sophisticated yet eminently danceable style. "I thought of them as really earthy, raw, real, meaningful songs with lots of variety," says Valerie Simpson. "The material was right on."

MFSB drummer Earl Young, who formed The Trammps just as Gamble & Huff launched Philadelphia International, was a central force to the sound. "My job in the studio with Kenny Gamble and them was to come in there with a groove," he says. "When they [Gamble & Huff] did 'Back Stabbers' or they gave me 'Love Train', they'd say, 'Earl, give me a groove for this.' They'd write notes and give me a chord chart but it was up to me on every song I recorded. Nobody wrote any grooves for me."

Young's playing on Harold Melvin & the Blue Notes' "The Love I Lost" marked a significant turning point in the kinds of grooves that appealed to discothèque audiences. "It wasn't the first disco groove but it was the first disco groove that hit the clubs like that," Young notes. His signature style also powered MFSB's "Love is the Message" and "TSOP (The Sound of Philadelphia)," which doubled as the theme to *Soul Train*—"That's a disco groove right there," he declares.

The range of soul, funk, and pop surfacing in the clubs during the early '70s kindled dance music's expansion throughout the decade. Artists and producers were already giving listeners new ways to move.

SLY & THE FAMILY STONE

In 1967, Sly & the Family Stone presaged the disco era with just four words: "Dance to the Music." The sentiment of the record—a rousing call to the dance floor, breaking down and spotlighting the instrumentation, a propulsive rhythm driving all the elements—would define countless records in the decade to come. Even the social fabric of clubs had a place in the groove. "All the squares go home," trumpet player Cynthia Robinson shouted at the climax, a witty progenitor to the velvet rope. ● However, Stone extolled a democratic philosophy in the group's late-'60s hits that captured the way discothèques brought different factions together. Somewhere between "I am everyday people" and "Everybody is a star," there was a sense of unity that magnified exponentially on the dance floor. And it all stemmed from the music. ● "Giving people energy was an interesting business," Stone observed decades later in his memoir. Indeed, his group's music set the soundtrack for Sanctuary, a club that was converted from the Second German Baptist Church in Hell's Kitchen, Manhattan. DJ historians Bill Brewster and Frank Broughton later called it "the first totally uninhibited gay discothèque in America" following the Stonewall Uprising in 1969. DJ Francis Grasso ruled from the pulpit, favoring a pair of songs that Stone wrote for other acts, including Little Sister's "You're the One" and Abaco Dream's "Life and Death in G & A." ● By the time Sly & the Family Stone topped the charts with "Family Affair" from *There's a Riot Goin' On* (1971)—the name was a response to Marvin Gaye's *What's Going On* (also 1971)—the group's leader had already colored outside the confines of AM radio-friendly singles. "Sex Machine" was a 13-minute groove from the group's 1969 *Stand!* album while "I Want to Take You Higher" was the ultimate rave-up. The self-proclaimed "Spaced Cowboy" had found new frontier, and he was about to have some company...

ISAAC HAYES

James Brown said it best: "Isaac Hayes is one of a kind." As a songwriter, producer, and session player for Stax Records in Memphis, Hayes had created some of the hottest records of the 1960s, including Sam & Dave's "Soul Man," before crowning the decade with his own musical statement, *Hot Buttered Soul* (1969). It was a sprawling masterpiece... and it featured only four cuts. ● Hayes' boundless approach to recording introduced a format that several producers would tailor for the discothèques (and the bedroom) throughout the 1970s, whether Giorgio Moroder & Pete Bellotte's production of "Love to Love You Baby" for Donna Summer or Cerrone's epic ode to ecstasy, "Love in C Minor." Only a visionary like Hayes could turn a three-letter word like "Joy" into a 16-minute experience. ● At the 1972 Academy Awards, Hayes won Best Original Song for "Theme from *Shaft*," thereby making history as the first Black musician to win an Oscar. He also popularized a symphonic musical style that would reverberate throughout the decade. Indeed, in September 1979, *Billboard* declared "Theme from Shaft" as "a forerunner of the funky but tight rhythms that would be labeled 'disco'". ● As disco swelled from the underground to the mainstream, Hayes tailored his signature style to the clubs. Tracks like "Chocolate Chip," "Disco Connection," "Groove-A-Thon," and "Don't Let Go" induced their own kind of fever. Disco pioneer Tom Moulton even mixed two of Hayes' most gripping productions, "Stranger in Paradise" from the Broadway musical *Timbuktu!* and the masterfully orchestrated "Moonlight Lovin' (Mènage a Trois)" for Hayes' Polydor debut, *New Horizon* (1977). ● "I've always been somewhat of a renegade," Hayes shared in an interview with Georgia Public Broadcasting. "Creatively, I dared to go where others feared to go." Isaac Hayes not only dared; he conquered.

New York City pulsed with the sound of Afro-rock during the early-'70s. Osibisa was the main source of ecstatic highs, especially with cuts like "Music for Gong Gong" and "Survival" masterfully woven into DJ sets by David Mancuso at The Loft or Francis Grasso at Sanctuary. This was not Motown, Memphis soul, or the Philly sound. This was an intoxicating blend of West African and Caribbean influences by way of London's rock scene. ● "We brought people together and made them happy," group founder Teddy Osei said to *The Guardian* 50 years after Osibisa released their self-titled debut in 1971. The group's name was derived from the "highlife" music based in Osei's home country, Ghana. "I called the group 'Osibisa' to reflect where the music came from—Fanti New Town in Kumasi—where all different kinds of music were developed," he added. Osei's musical vision was global. He led a seven-member group that included fellow Ghanians—Sol Amarfio and Mac Tontoh—plus Lasisi Amao (Nigeria), Spartacus R (Grenada), Wendell Richardson (Antigua), and Robert Bailey (Trinidad). ● Osibisa's first two albums for MCA Records were Top 20 hits in the UK as Afro-rock crossed the Atlantic. Writing in *Rolling Stone*, Vince Aletti recommended the group's second album *Woyaya* (1972) for any readers wanting to start a "discothèque library" based on what DJs were spinning in the clubs. *Billboard* magazine was also taking notes, writing in December 1972, "The music is perhaps the first original contribution initiated by Britain's African and West Indian population—with few influences derived from American soul/R&B or West Indian reggae. Afro-rock instead is a blend of Western rock and African rhythms." ● "Our ethos was happy music and good vibes," Osei [pictured center] said years later. For the sense of freedom permeating New York, Osibisa offered a simpatico sound.

MFSB

Disco was crystalized with four letters—MFSB. ● Producers Kenny Gamble and Leon Huff, with producer and arranger Thom Bell, presided over more than two dozen musicians at Philadelphia's Sigma Sound Studios. With engineer Joe Tarsia at the helm, MFSB (Mother Father Sister Brother) provided the musical foundation of early club favorites like "Love Train" by The O'Jays, and Harold Melvin & the Blue Notes' "The Love I Lost," among countless other hits for Gamble and Huff's Philadelphia International Records (PIR), not to mention Bell's productions for groups like The Delfonics, The Stylistics, and The Spinners. ● MFSB's own album, *Love is the Message* (1973), delivered two anthems for the burgeoning disco scene. Featuring guest vocals by The Three Degrees, "TSOP (The Sound of Philadelphia)" not only doubled as the theme to *Soul Train*, but also topped the pop and R&B charts in 1974, and won a GRAMMY Award for "Best R&B Instrumental Performance." The Three Degrees also appeared on "Love is the Message," which became the anthem for The Loft, especially after Tom Moulton remixed the track for Gamble and Huff's *Philadelphia Classics* (1977) collection. *Pitchfork* has even called it "The most important disco record ever." ● Individual MFSB players were prolific in their own disco projects beyond Philly International. Vibraphonist Vincent Montana, Jr. created, produced, and conducted The Salsoul Orchestra, which scored several hits including "Nice 'n' Naasty," "Magic Bird of Fire," "Love Break (Ooh I Love It)," and a cover of "Tangerine," plus records with Charo ("Dance a Little Bit Closer") and Loleatta Holloway ("Run Away"). Drummer and producer Earl Young, who *The Guardian* later called "the architect of the disco beat," became one of disco's MVPs as both a member of The Trammps and a frequent collaborator with MFSB players Norman Harris (guitar) and Ronnie Baker (bass). ● Though more than one song sparked the disco phenomenon, MFSB certainly shaped a prototype for the sound. "If you listen back to all those records we were doing then, you'll hear that 4/4 time," Thom Bell noted about MFSB's impact. "They were the forerunners. There was no disco music before." ● "We were there at the *right* time."

THE TEMPTATIONS

The Temptations heard their future when they heard Sly & the Family Stone. Motown producer Norman Whitfield helped them translate the propulsive energy of Sly's "Dance to the Music" into their own late-'60s hit, "Cloud Nine," sparking The Temptations' venture towards psychedelic soul. ● Whitfield further expanded The Temptations' sound to widescreen dimensions over the next few albums. *All Directions* (1972) introduced a new iteration of the group—[left to right] Melvin Franklin, Dennis Edwards, Otis Williams, Damon Harris, and Richard Street—as "Papa Was a Rolling Stone" topped the pop chart and won three GRAMMY Awards. It was a remarkable triumph, given how the 12-minute track was edited down to seven minutes for the single release, more than double the length of the singles on AM radio. ● "We never thought it would ever get played," recalled Edwards, speaking to *Soul Cellar* in 2000. "The [radio] jocks had not really gotten together on whether or not to play long records. We were the top group in the world. We came out with it and said, 'This is our new record.' So we made them play it. After that, a lot of groups came out with longer-playing records. It was that driving beat, that haunting beat for that era." ● The Temptations solidified their club appeal with "Law of the Land" from *Masterpiece* (1973). With its thunderous, hypnotic rhythm, it was a natural for club play, joining former Temptations vocalist Eddie Kendricks' "Girl You Need a Change of Mind" as one of the era's most celebrated tracks. The group continued to sate club appetites with producer Jeffrey Bowen on *A Song for You* (1975). The tight, streamlined bounce of "Happy People," "Glasshouse," and "Shakey Ground" was irresistible. Dennis Edwards said it perfectly: "We were in a great groove at that time."

MANU DIBANGO

August 1973. Manu Dibango makes his North American debut at the Apollo Theater in Harlem. It's the first night of his ten-day residency. "Soul Makossa" is storming up the charts thanks to DJ Frankie Crocker at WBLS. Dibango shares the bill with The Temptations, but the audience turns their attention towards the newly arrived saxophone player from Cameroon. ● "The Temptations were the stars of the moment, but people didn't come for them," Dibango later recalled. "They really wanted to see the African band [*laughs*]. The spectators arrived with maracas, tambourines... they made the rhythm in the room. From the first measurements of 'Soul Makossa,' it made them crazy." ● Dibango had followed a circuitous route to the Apollo. Just a year earlier, he'd recorded "Soul Makossa" in France, mixing together American R&B with "makossa," a style of music and dance from Dibango's home city, Douala. "For me, it was natural to play like that," he recalled. "We used a double bass line, and we doubled the drums too. On top of that, the drummer was left-handed, and it created a shift—there were no drum machines back then. These were all the elements that made up this magical rhythm." ● Those elements appealed to David Mancuso's sensibilities. He spun an import copy of "Soul Makossa" at The Loft and, almost overnight, the record coursed through countless New York clubs. By June 1973, *Billboard* reported that no less than seven record companies had released their own versions of "Soul Makossa" while Atlantic Records negotiated with Société Française du Son to license Dibango's original recording for the US market. ● "I treat music like painting," Dibango explained years later. "I learned to orchestrate and mix sounds and instruments—to marry colors together." Indeed, the colors in "Soul Makossa" created a vibrant kaleidoscope of rhythm.

"I never went to a place full of these people, who as a group, would lose it over a song. Their reactions represented the ultimate freedom," DJ Danny Krivit said in an interview with *NPR*. The place was The Loft. The song was "City, Country, City" by WAR. ● "If you don't make people dance, they can't relate to it," declares original WAR drummer Harold Brown. WAR's music defied categorization. The band constantly experimented with different rhythms and infused their albums with musical influences from across the globe. "We grew up in a multicultural environment, hearing all types of music," adds Brown. "We were listening to James Brown, the boogaloo, Johnny Otis. We were always hearing those *clave* things and boleros." ● The seven-piece group from Long Beach, California, who began their recording career as the backing band for Animals frontman Eric Burdon ("Spill the Wine"), had several hits to their name by the time they recorded "City, Country, City" for *The World is a Ghetto* (1972). Beyond the clubs, the album topped the pop and R&B charts. *Billboard* deemed it the "Number One Album of 1973." ● WAR even brought Latin-spiced funk to outer space on the title track to *Galaxy* (1977), which *Record World* described as "Part *Star Wars*, part tribal rite, part jazz jam, part house party." The track's unique rhythm rocketed through the clubs. "I learned how to play the *batucada*, Brazilian music," Brown notes about the rhythm. "I was trying to play that in the studio. Different people laid their parts down. I remember standing by [producer] Jerry Goldstein. We listened to the first part of it. I looked at Jerry and I said [*sings*] 'Take me to your place in space. I'm sick and tired of the rat race.'" ● Dancers heeded WAR's spacey invocation. The consensus? "It's outta sight!"

THE INTRUDERS

August 19, 1973. The Intruders are performing for nearly 100,000 fans at Watts Summer Festival in Los Angeles. Robert "Big Sonny" Edwards, Phil Terry, Eugene "Bird" Daughtry, and lead vocalist Sam "Little Sonny" Brown [right] bring a sweet dose of Philly soul to the concert. "I'll Always Love My Mama" is their latest hit off *Save the Children* (1973). Miles away in New York, DJ Nicky Siano is spinning the song at The Gallery. It's a cool breeze through the hot summer heat of the city. ● "The Intruders were a Philadelphia favorite," says Kenny Gamble, who penned "I'll Always Love My Mama" with Leon Huff, Gene McFadden, and John Whitehead in tribute to his mother. Gamble had first heard The Intruders more than 10 years earlier on their recording "Come Home Soon" (1961). "It was beautiful," he said. "I can remember going to see The Intruders at a rock and roll show at the Dell Theatre... I said, 'That's my favorite group.'" ● In fact, The Intruders were the first act that Gamble and Huff produced on their Excel/Gamble label in 1966, five years before the team launched Philadelphia International Records (PIR). No less a powerhouse than The Temptations praised the group in the liner notes to the back cover of the quartet's *Cowboys to Girls* (1968). The title track topped the R&B chart and earned the group a gold single, foreshadowing the success Gamble and Huff would have with their roster of artists in the coming decade. ● However, it was The Intruders' single "She's A Winner" (1972) that helped define the danceable, sweeping sound of Philadelphia International. Shrouded by MFSB's string section, with drummer Earl Young driving the beat, the record was more than a "winner," it was Philly soul perfection.

EDDIE KENDRICKS

"What you say to that?" Anyone visiting a discothèque in the early-'70s would likely have those words seared into their soul. The hook from Eddie Kendricks' "Girl You Need a Change of Mind" was like a rallying call in the clubs. With the release of his 1972 solo album *People... Hold On*, the former Temptations vocalist's rousing falsetto, which led classics like "Get Ready" and "Just My Imagination (Running Away with Me)," kept dancers on the floor till sunrise. ● "I wanted to move away from the Motown sound and get closer to what people were hearing when Eddie played live. We got that live feel with 'Girl You Need a Change of Mind,'" said producer Frank Wilson, who created the song's eight-minute groove. The record featured two breakdowns that gave DJs space to deftly blend in and out of other tracks. "My background is the church," Wilson continued. "It's not unusual in a church song to have a breakdown like that. I stood out in the studio with the musicians, giving instructions as we were cutting for them to break it down to nothing, then gradually come in one by one and rebuild to the original fervor of the song." ● "Girl You Need a Change of Mind," plus Wilson's bewitching production of "Date With the Rain," prefigured Kendricks' biggest solo records, the chart-topping "Keep On Truckin'" and "Boogie Down." In 1976, producer and MFSB guitarist Norman Harris, who crafted hits for The Trammps, First Choice, and Double Exposure, bolstered Kendricks' club profile with another pair of hits, "He's a Friend" and "Goin' Up in Smoke." It was the perfect marriage of Motown with the Philly sound. ● "I'm putting out feeling," Kendricks told *Billboard* in 1973. "Everybody understands feeling. Only thing they can do is fight the feeling." Whenever Kendricks' voice towered above the grooves, crowds willingly surrendered to that feeling.

HAROLD MELVIN & THE BLUE NOTES

Harold Melvin & the Blue Notes, plus MFSB, plus a song by Kenny Gamble and Leon Huff, equaled disco perfection. Though "disco" had yet to become common parlance in 1973, "The Love I Lost" launched a thousand nights of dance floor bliss. ● "'The Love I Lost' was gonna be a ballad," says MFSB drummer Earl Young. "I changed it to an up-tempo in the studio. It was my four-on-the-floor. It fit so well in there that Gamble okayed for me to use it. He said, "I love it. This is what we're going to do.'" At the time, Billboard noted just how essential Young was to the six-minute track: "The almost irresistibly catchy beat, with its strutting effect, proved to set off the entire piece and made it a natural for the rapidly more important, back-to-dancing market." ● Lead vocalist Teddy Pendergrass was a mighty force, however. "He had this tremendous voice that just wouldn't be denied," says Valerie Simpson. "Teddy does reach the bottom of your soul because he connects with you," adds legendary mix-master Tom Moulton. "It's magical. When he sang something, you believed that he experienced it." The singer's impassioned approach would drive the best of the Blue Notes, including "Where Are All My Friends" and "Tell the World How I Feel About 'Cha Baby," nearly as much as the rhythm. ● By 1975, the disco market had been established and Harold Melvin & the Blue Notes scored the year's biggest club hit, with "Bad Luck" topping Record World's disco chart for eight weeks. "The energy of that song was very uplifting, almost in a religious way," says Moulton, who would subsequently expand "Bad Luck" and the group's bracing version of "Don't Leave Me This Way." Teddy Pendergrass embarked on a solo career a year later, but disco was far from finished with him...

MARVIN GAYE

The early 1970s needed Marvin Gaye. *What's Going On* (1971) was a powerful response to the social unrest of the time, especially the Vietnam War. During the summer of 1971, the title track left dancers on Fire Island (the ultimate sandbox for New York's gay community) completely spellbound. "'What's Going On' was *the* song," photographer Richard Brezner recalled in Tim Lawrence's book *Love Saves the Day* (2004). "When it was played in the Sandpiper everyone would hug and sway. The warmth of the music, the romantic sounds—it all embodied Fire Island Pines." ● "Marvin made me know the power of the spoken word," explained Donna Summer. "As a freedom fighter and songwriter, Marvin Gaye had the soul of a revolutionary drenched in the passion of a poet. It seemed every word was gleaned and processed through the spectrum of love, desire, and pain. There is an urgency in his music that resounds in every heart that has ever heard it." ● Gaye asserted his creative independence at Motown with *What's Going On* and, as the decade progressed, *Let's Get It On* (1973) and *I Want You* (1976) further attested to his brilliance. Though Gaye's records had long been catnip for DJs, dating back to 1968's "I Heard It Through the Grapevine," he resisted any obvious commercial concessions to the disco format. However, by the end of 1976, Motown persuaded Gaye to record his own nod to the disco phenomenon—"Got to Give It Up." ● Conceptually, "Got to Give It Up" was the link between a record that partly inspired Gaye—Johnnie Taylor's "Disco Lady"—and The Jacksons' "Shake Your Body (Down to the Ground)," which lifted "let's dance, let's shout" from Gaye's song. *Record World* called the 12-minute track "downright hypnotic" as it topped the pop, R&B, and disco charts. Not even wallflowers could resist Gaye's command to "dance all night."

QUINCY JONES

In the early '70s, DJs looking to surprise their audience might have gone to one of music's greatest maestros—Quincy Jones. His cover of the celestial "Walking in Space" from the musical *Hair*, as well as Motown hits like "What's Going On," and Stevie Wonder's "Superstition," offered palate cleansers from the originals, with adventurous DJs perhaps even blending the different versions. ● Jones began hitting a stride with jazz-infused funk during the mid '70s with "Boogie Joe, the Grinder" from *Body Heat* (1974), plus his production for The Brothers Johnson's debut, *Look Out for #1* (1976). The duo made the disco Top 20 with "Get the Funk Out Ma Face," which A&M Records championed as "one of the year's biggest disco/R&B smashes." ● Two years later, Jones brought together Ashford & Simpson, Chaka Khan, and members of New York band Stuff for one of the era's cleverest odes to hedonism, "Stuff Like That." As Valerie Simpson, who'd also sung on Jones' renditions of "Walking in Space" and "What's Going On," recalls: "Quincy sent us the track and we came up with that feeling... All the guys that were on the track are dear, dear friends and raucous and just crazy and fun. We had worked together, all of us, many, many times, so it was like a family thing. That was just a fun assignment." ● Jones capped the decade with some of his greatest success in the discos, producing Rufus & Chaka Khan's *Masterjam* (1979), which featured the incendiary "Any Love," and Michael Jackson's *Off the Wall* (1979). Of course, the latter album also became one of the most successful albums of the year with the chart-topping "Don't Stop 'Til You Get Enough" and "Rock With You," plus essential album tracks like "Get on the Floor." No matter the record, musical excellence could be defined by a single letter in the alphabet—"Q."

THE O'JAYS

Get down and get on board! The O'Jays were among the groups to premiere Kenny Gamble and Leon Huff's Philadelphia International Records. Members [left to right] Eddie Levert, Walter Williams, and William Powell became a signature act for the company with their debut for the label, *Back Stabbers* (1972). The album heralded a new era of success for the trio while furnishing clubs with hits like "Love Train," "Time to Get Down," and the haunting title track. ● "We learned that *Back Stabbers* album where I could have done it in my sleep," Eddie Levert recalls. "We rehearsed it every day until we knew the songs backwards and forwards. Very few songs you know before they go out the door that they're going to be hit records, but with [the title track] 'Back Stabbers,' we knew we were on our way." ● "Love Train" brought The O'Jays to the top of the pop and R&B charts, while also becoming a mainstay in clubs. The track's chugging groove cushioned an optimistic anthem of unity during a time of discord. "There were a lot of social issues, riots, and there were a lot of wounds that needed to be healed as far as being a Black person in the USA," Walter Williams recalls. "Gamble and Huff were writers about situations like that. I guess we were the messengers because we were the guys that sang the songs—'When the World's at Peace,' 'Give the People What They Want,' 'For the Love of Money,' 'Love Train,' all of these things were on people's minds." ● Gamble and Huff also captured the intrinsic joy of the discos with "I Love Music." Beginning in November 1975, The O'Jays' dynamic performance kept "I Love Music" at number one on the disco chart for eight consecutive weeks. Whether enjoining listeners to "Put Your Hands Together" or board the "Love Train," The O'Jays were the consummate ambassadors of the Philadelphia sound.

THE O'JAYS
PUT YOUR HANDS

THE ISLEY BROTHERS

The Isley Brothers had been forces in dance music ever since the late-'50s. "Shout" put an exclamation point on 1959, while their version of "Twist and Shout" (1962) turned any gathering into an instant party. Following their tenure at Motown, where they recorded the definitive version of Holland-Dozier-Holland's "This Old Heart of Mine (Is Weak for You)," The Isley Brothers emerged as funk titans on their own label, T-Neck. Their first release, "It's Your Thing," topped the R&B chart and won a GRAMMY for Best R&B Vocal Performance by a Duo or Group. ● The band greeted the 1970s with *Get Into Something* (1970), with the title track landing in New York clubs like The Gallery and Tamburlaine. Three years later, *3+3* (1973) unveiled a new six-member lineup, bridging the Isley vocal trio—Ronald [center], Rudolph [second from right], and O'Kelly [second from left]—with younger brothers Ernie [right], Melvin [left], and brother-in-law Chris Jasper [standing center]. In remodeling "Who's That Lady?" (1964) for the 1970s, they fused soul, rock, and dance, characterized by Ernie Isley's blistering guitar. "When I hit the first note on 'That Lady,' the song went from black and white to 3-D technology," he told *PopMatters* in 2015. ● "That Lady" was certified gold and brought The Isley Brothers back to the Top Five of the R&B chart, yet the distributing partner of their record company was initially uncertain about where to place the single. "The very first time we played it for CBS [Records], they said, 'It doesn't sound like 'It's Your Thing,'" Ernie later shared in an interview with Arts Fuse. "'We like it, and it's got a lot of elements to it—dance, R&B, the guitar tone—it's quite dynamic but we don't know how we should market it.' And our response was, 'Just put it out! Let it go everywhere.' We were in pursuit of the music... When it turned into the different records and styles, there was a sense of surprise and discovery and celebration on our part." And with "That Lady" leading the way for "Live It Up," "Fight the Power," and "The Pride," The Isley Brothers' discovery yielded one classic after another.

1974–1975

It's the summer of 1975 and disco fever is ablaze in New York. Diana Ross is sitting with Andy Warhol. She recently went club hopping with Cher and Bette Midler and is regaling Warhol with the details during a conversation for *Interview Magazine*. "You wouldn't believe the places we went!" she exclaims. "We just walked in and the three of us just got on the floor and started to dance and the people went absolutely insane! We started out at Le Jardin... and then we went down to the Village to somewhere across from where Bette lives. Then we zapped up Elton (John) and he was with us and the four of us started runnin' around."

New York Magazine hailed Le Jardin as "among the most beautiful of all dance halls, a steamy exotica of swirling lights" nestled inside the Hotel Diplomat. Resident DJ Bobby Guttadaro held dancers rapt that summer with MFSB ("Sexy"), People's Choice ("Do It Any Way You Wanna"), The Ritchie Family ("Brazil"), South Shore Commission ("Free Man"), and a song that Ross herself had originated with The Supremes, "Forever Came Today," completely revamped by The Jackson 5 for the discothèques.

A year before, disco had ascended from the clubs to the top of the pop charts. Barry White's Love Unlimited Orchestra scored a number one hit with "Love's Theme" in February 1974, followed by MFSB's "TSOP (The Sound of Philadelphia)" in April. The summer of 1974, however, marked an important moment for disco's emergence in the pop realm when two records took consecutive turns at the top, "Rock the Boat" by The Hues Corporation and "Rock Your Baby" by George McCrae. "I'd give my eyetooth to have written that," John Lennon later said about the latter song, underscoring the regard that even the most lauded pop songwriters had for the form.

Trade magazines began measuring club play as *Billboard* magazine launched its "Disco Action" chart in October 1974 and Vince Aletti began writing his "Disco File" column for *Record World* the following month. Gloria Gaynor's "Never Can Say Goodbye" had the distinction as the first number one disco hit. For the singer's full-length debut, produced by Meco Monardo, Tony Bongiovi, and Jay Ellis, Tom Moulton blended the song with "Honey Bee" and "Reach Out, I'll Be There" in one uninterrupted suite. "I had this idea to put these three songs together," says Moulton. "I was very much into storytelling and one thing leading into the next." Gaynor applauded his genius: "I was all for that because I loved dancing," she says. "As far as remixes were concerned, Tom was the king in knowing how to keep you on the dance floor."

"Tom is really the man," says legendary DJ Nicky Siano, who owed The Gallery. "He really changed the way records were being mixed. I think his sound was just a very pure club sound that no one else had really developed." Moulton also pioneered the extended "disco break" on Don Downing's single "Dream World," stripping back the vocals and instrumentation while drums and percussion drove the track forward. That same year, his mix of "I'll Be Holding On" by Al Downing revolutionized the process of pressing promotional singles on 12-inch vinyl, which standardized a format that offered optimal sound quality and playback in the discos.

Scepter Records, which released "Dream World," received *Billboard*'s Trendsetter of the Year Award in December 1974 for "being the first label to make specialized mixes for discothèques." Led by "Dream World," Scepter released a series of singles with mixes for both radio and the discos, notably Ultra High Frequency's "We're on the Right Track," and "(Do It) Till You're Satisfied" by B.T. Express.

"Radio is spreading disco music faster than ever before," *Record World* duly noted in March 1975. Several key tracks crowned the pop chart. Established funk and R&B acts like Labelle, Ohio Players, and Earth, Wind & Fire scored number one pop hits with club-tested material while KC & the Sunshine Band pumped out a pair of number ones on T.K. Records, "Get Down Tonight" and "That's the Way (I Like It)." In fact, T.K. put Miami on the map with popular cuts by Betty Wright and George McCrae while the city's famed Criteria Studios was home base for the Bee Gees' resurgence with "Jive Talkin'."

However, it was Van McCoy who captured an international dance phenomenon with his chart-topping homage to "The Hustle" in 1975. "I was introduced to the hustle by a disc jockey [David Todd] at a New York City nightclub called the Adam's Apple," McCoy later told *Billboard*. "He'd been after me for a while to come and check out this new dance, but I just never had the chance, so I sent one of my friends. When he came back, he showed me this very strange dance. It was something completely different from the you-do-your-thing-and-I-do-mine dances; it was people dancing together again. It reminded me of ballroom dancing, and I love graceful dancing." The dance itself would inspire additional club hits that same year, including "Salsoul Hustle" by The Salsoul Orchestra and Eddie Drennon's "Let's Do the Latin Hustle."

Four thousand miles away in Munich, a new sound had surfaced in the studios. German group Silver Convention introduced a sleek and streamlined groove with sweeping orchestral melodies on "Fly, Robin, Fly," illustrating the key elements that would characterize disco as a genre. Following the single's chart-topping triumph on the pop, R&B, and disco charts in 1975, *Record World* columnist Vince Aletti noted how "The success of Silver Convention's ecstatic 'Fly, Robin, Fly' could not have come a year or two ago—before the preconditioning of Barry White, George McCrae, MFSB, and Bohannon—and more than any other song this year, it's an indication that the style and spirit of disco have taken hold and begun changing popular taste significantly."

Musically, "Fly, Robin, Fly" prepared audiences for another Munich-based artist who was about to conquer popular music across the board—Donna Summer. Produced and co-written with Giorgio Moroder and Pete Bellotte, the singer's 17-minute "Love to Love You Baby" filled the entire side of an album. "This was a new high in terms of sustained music," says Aletti. "The first time I heard it played was at a meeting for the record pool, which was in David Mancuso's Loft space on Prince Street. A DJ who had gotten an advance copy brought it into play and everybody freaked out. It was just a breakthrough in terms of length—the sensuality that Donna Summer brought to the record and then this kind of heightened, very intense music that kept driving and building and really had a shape to it."

Signed to Casablanca Records in Los Angeles, Donna Summer returned to the US after seven years in Munich and experienced the rush of sudden superstardom. "I flew into New York at some point to do the press junket that they had put together for me," she recalled. "I went to all the major cities across the United States. I had never done anything like that, which was get on the plane, go to these discothèques, pump up everything, have parties... then we were on a plane going to the next stop." After Summer scored her first number one disco hit in October 1975, the progression of her career over the next five years would mirror dance music's own evolution.

Beyond all expectations, dance music, and disco specifically, was about to become a multi-billion-dollar industry.

BARRY WHITE

"We got it together." A low rumble echoed throughout clubs in 1974. The sound was the ultimate voice of seduction—Barry White. His opening rap on "You're the First, the Last, My Everything" topped a confection of strings that whipped around the beat. It doubled as an entrée to dancing... and making love. ● White's Love Unlimited Orchestra was a wellspring of symphonic rhapsodies for both his solo recordings and his vocal trio, Love Unlimited. Legendary arranger Gene Page helped articulate White's vision, conducting a 40-piece orchestra that rivaled MFSB as one of disco's greatest symphonies. When Love Unlimited Orchestra's "Love's Theme" crowned the Hot 100 in February 1974, it made history as one of the first records to earn the number one spot almost entirely as a result of its popularity on the dancefloor. ● Written and produced by White, "Love's Theme" swept dancers up into a swirl of romance. However, 20th Century Records nearly overlooked the song, only putting it out as a single after DJ Nicky Siano began spinning the record at his downtown club, The Gallery. The record company even awarded DJ Bobby Guttadaro a gold record for his effort in breaking "Love's Theme" at Le Jardin in New York's Hotel Diplomat, signaling the music industry's growing awareness in how vital clubs were to selling records. ● Throughout the decade, White furnished variations on his Love Unlimited formula. In 1976, Love Unlimited Orchestra's "My Sweet Summer Suite" topped the disco chart for three weeks. The following year, White's "It's Ecstasy When You Lay Down Next to Me" revitalized his profile in the discos and inspired one of 1977's most contagious club grooves, "Le Spank" by Le Pamplemousse. Though records by other artists left little to the imagination, the Maestro of Love continued to arouse listeners with just a simple caress... and a "Love's Theme" for all time.

BARRY
LOVE

THE THREE DEGREES

The Three Degrees brought glamour, beauty, and pristine harmonies to Philadelphia International Records. Produced by Kenny Gamble and Leon Huff, their 1973 debut for PIR spawned two years' worth of hits everywhere from Japan to Germany, including number ones in Holland ("Dirty Ol' Man") and the UK ("When Will I See You Again"). ● "We didn't know that 'When Will I See You Again' was going to be a number one for us. We just thought it was a nice ballad," says Valerie Holiday [center], whose crystal-clear blend with Sheila Ferguson [right] and Fayette Pinkney [left] sparkled on every song. "You have to go in with each song on that positive note so, just in case, you know that you gave it your best shot." ● On the home front, "I Didn't Know" climbed the R&B chart while Nicky Siano added "Dirty Ol' Man" to his repertoire at The Gallery. The trio's guest vocals on MFSB's "Love is the Message" and "TSOP (The Sound of Philadelphia)" assured them a permanent place in disco's pantheon. "We view disco in a different way," Holiday explains. "We were still R&B. It may have been 'disco' but it still had a solid back beat to it." ● Boldly shifting course in 1978, The Three Degrees recorded two albums with Giorgio Moroder, whose electronic sensibilities gave them an edgier sound on *New Dimensions* (1978) and *3D* (1979). "We had to maintain some type of visibility within the market so that automatically demands that you change," says Holiday, who welcomed original member Helen Scott back into the trio as the lineup evolved with their sound. The group closed the '70s with two major disco hits in Europe, "Giving Up, Giving In" and "The Runner," plus the rock and disco fusion of "Jump the Gun" and "Red Light." From Gamble and Huff to Moroder, The Three Degrees thrived within the full scope of the era's greatest innovators.

"The Mother of Hip Hop." Pioneering record producer. Rock and Roll Hall of Fame honoree. Queen of boudoir soul. Only one person can claim it all—Sylvia Robinson. ● Years before she entranced listeners with "Pillow Talk" in 1973, Sylvia established her career as a singer, songwriter, and producer, especially as one half of Mickey & Sylvia ("Love is Strange"). In 1968, Sylvia and her husband Joe Robinson founded the independent label, All Platinum Records. She produced the chart-topping "Love on a Two-Way Street" for The Moments in 1970 and scored her own number one solo hit with "Pillow Talk" three years later. Sylvia had offered the erotically charged anthem to Al Green before approaching it from a woman's point of view. "I just wanted to say things that women wanted to say but were afraid to," she told *Dazed* years later. "I sang about sexy thoughts and fantasies." ● A jolt of galloping grooves powered Sylvia's next chart-topping smash, "Shame, Shame, Shame" (1974), which she wrote and produced for Shirley & Company on All Platinum's Vibration label. Two decades earlier, the song's lead vocalist Shirley Goodman had made jukebox favorite "Let the Good Times Roll," as part of Shirley & Lee. "Shame, Shame, Shame" spent four weeks at number one on *Billboard*'s Disco Action chart in January 1975 and reached the Top 10 in nearly a dozen countries across the globe. However, Sylvia broke ground when she co-founded Sugar Hill Records in 1979 and produced "Rapper's Delight" by The Sugarhill Gang, hastening hip hop's rise as a commercial force in the 1980s. Whether it was rap, disco, or a sweet dose of sumptuously orchestrated soul, Sylvia always took it to the top.

JOE BATAAN

"You're a bridge to many cultures," a curator for the Smithsonian told Joe Bataan when the esteemed cultural institution honored him in 2010. Born to Black and Filipino parents, and raised in East Harlem's predominantly Puerto Rican neighborhood, Bataan became the "King of Latin Soul" during the 1960s by pairing English lyrics with the Latin rhythms he heard echoing through streets and fire escapes. ● After recording several albums for the legendary Fania label, Bataan signed with Mericana Records and introduced a phrase to the lexicon of dance music on his first album for the company, *Salsoul* (1974). "Salsoul was my name," he says. "I originated it, and I started it. 'Sal' is short for salsa. 'Soul,' of course, is soul." Powered by "Latin Strut," *Salsoul* topped *Billboard*'s "Hot Latin Albums" chart during the summer of 1974. ● *Salsoul* doubled as the name of the new label Bataan created with Mericana owners Joe, Ken, and Stan Cayre. In January 1975, Salsoul Records officially launched with Bataan's instrumental rendition of Gil Scott-Heron's "The Bottle," featuring David Sanborn on saxophone. "The beat is infectious," he says. "I glorified the record with strings and horns and gave it the excitement of an instrumental. It was done in one take. We knew right away that this was going to be a hit. Quiet as it's kept, I was one of the few artists in New York that knew how to push a record in clubs. I went to every disc jockey in New York. They played 'The Bottle' back-to-back with Gil Scott-Heron in all the discos." Bataan's instincts were infallible. "The Bottle" landed in the Top 5 of the disco chart and gave Salsoul Records the first of countless club hits. ● From Spanish Harlem to the Smithsonian, Bataan blazed a trail of sizzling grooves.

FIRST CHOICE

From their earliest albums, First Choice found fans in everyone from *Soul Train* host Don Cornelius to celebrated musicians like Stevie Wonder. "We played the Copacabana in New York," recalls lead vocalist and group founder Rochelle Fleming [center]. "Stevie came to the show. He started singing 'Smarty Pants.' I stopped the band. This was how fresh my little mouth was. I said, 'Excuse me Stevie. This is *First Choice's* show! The audience cracked up." ● Wonder could hardly resist singing along with the Philly-based trio, who *Record World* once named "Top Disco Girl Group." Since debuting in 1972 with "This is the House (Where Loved Died)" on Scepter Records, First Choice had become a source of powerful grooves typified by their work with producer and MFSB guitarist Norman Harris. "We did other songs that other girl groups wouldn't have sung," Fleming says. Indeed, the title tracks to *Armed and Extremely Dangerous* (1973) and *The Player* (1974) were essential additions to any DJ's repertoire at the time, distinguishing First Choice from their contemporaries with bold, dramatic storylines. ● Signing with Salsoul Records via Norman Harris' Gold Mind label, *Delusions* (1977) was their masterpiece. As well as a cover of Stevie Wonder and Syreeta's "Love Having You Around," the album introduced classics like "Doctor Love" and "Let No Man Put Asunder," with the latter cut's infectious refrain "it's not over" becoming a mantra for the clubs. They crowned the '70s with "Love Thang" and "Double Cross" from *Hold Your Horses* (1979) featuring a cover illustration by *Interview* magazine's Richard Bernstein. WBLS DJ Frankie Crocker, another of the trio's many admirers, had a special surprise for the group upon the album's release. "When we did Studio 54, Frankie Crocker had heard about 'Hold Your Horses,'" says Fleming. "He came in Studio 54 on a white horse. This man adored First Choice and we felt the same way about him." ● Tracing an entire decade of dance music's progression, "First Choice" was a perfect appellation for the group.

KOOL & THE GANG

"Spirit of the Boogie" was more than a number one song for Kool & the Gang. It was a musical manifesto. Their fusion of jazz and funk had fueled million-selling hits like "Jungle Boogie" and "Hollywood Swinging," tracks that belonged to the clubs as much as the pop charts. In fact, Kool & the Gang had their own "Boogie Man" who gave the group a distinctive personality—Donal Boyce [third from left]. ● "Don started out as our sound and lighting person," Robert "Kool" Bell [fourth from left] explained in the liner notes to a 2011 *Open Sesame* reissue. "Then he began making the 'boogie' sounds while he was performing his various functions at the board. We brought him in to be the Boogie Man on 'Jungle Boogie' for the *Wild and Peaceful* (1973) album." Boyce appeared on several more tracks, including his indelible appearance as the Genie on *Open Sesame*'s title track (1976). ● "'Open Sesame' was the brainchild of Mr. Ronald Bell (Khalis Bayyan)," recalled sax player Dennis "Dee Tee" Thomas [second from right]. "It's magnificent." Drummer George Brown added, "We were very young, had a lot of notoriety and were refusing to just continue along without growing and expanding our sound. 'Open Sesame' was my first time incorporating a four-on-the-floor drumming technique for the rhythm, which is four quarter notes on bass drum and two beats over it. That took the intricate horn parts and the funky groove to a relatable, danceable level." A year later, the grandeur of "Open Sesame" memorably shone on the soundtrack to *Saturday Night Fever* (1977). ● By decade's end, *Ladies Night* (1979), their first album with lead vocalist James "J.T." Taylor and producer Eumir Deodato, ushered Kool & the Gang into the most commercially successful period of their career and led the way to platinum pop anthems like "Celebration"... but it all began with the boogie.

HOHNER

THE JIMMY CASTOR BUNCH

There's a reason why Jimmy Castor was dubbed the Everything Man. As a songwriter, producer, singer, bandleader, and multi-instrumentalist, he did *everything*. He even turned the moniker into a superhero, memorably illustrated comic-book-style on the album covers for *Butt of Course* (1974) and *Supersound* (1975). ● It was the latest character in a universe populated by figures from Castor's songs: the million-selling "Troglodyte (Cave Man)," "Luther the Anthropoid," Bertha from "The Bertha Butt Boogie," and the recurring "Leroy" character introduced on Castor's first Top 40 hit, the Latin-influenced "Hey, Leroy, Your Mama's Callin' You" (1966). ● Castor brought a sense of humor to his albums, preceding George Clinton's own character inventions in Parliament, yet his musicality was the height of sophistication. Playing soprano saxophone and timbales, Castor led a six-piece band shaped by the blend of musical influences from his childhood in Harlem and Washington Heights. "I wanted to appeal to the masses," he told *The Quietus* years later. "I'm a pop-funk act with lots of Latin because of Tito Puente, Ricardo Ray, Joe Cuba. I learned from them." ● The title track to Castor's RCA debut *It's Just Begun* (1972) reflected a musical and social perspective that surfaced in everything from disco to hip hop. "We were doing a lot of discos then," Castor noted. "We made a thing that would reach everyone. 'Day or night, Black and white'—that's *everybody*. When I did that, it came from the pyramids. You could hear the ground moving, like when Sly did 'Higher.'" ● With its riveting polyrhythms, "It's Just Begun" emerged as a foundational record for b-boys and breakdancers, becoming a widely sourced track among 3,000 samples from Castor's catalog. However, the reason for Castor's enduring influence could be explained by one of his own credos: "A Groove Will Make You Move."

THE HUES CORPORATION

The Hues Corporation sailed to number one on the Hot 100 with "Rock the Boat" during the summer of 1974. The track's buoyant rhythm drove the irresistible call-and-response between lead vocalist Fleming Williams [pictured left] and group members St. Clair Lee and H. Ann Kelley. Were it not for discothèques, however, The Hues Corporation might have been lost at sea. ● Even the trio's label had little faith in the record, the third single off their RCA debut, *Freedom for the Stallion* (1973). "The record came out some time in February (1974) and it's fair to say that by the middle of March, it was totally dead," recalls group manager, Wally Holmes. "Suddenly, when the record wasn't on any radio station, it sold 50,000 copies in New York City." New York clubs had kept "Rock the Boat" in circulation, proving the previously untapped power of clubs to sell tens of thousands of records without radio play. ● At the time, *New York Magazine* selected "Rock the Boat" to characterize a fresh crop of club-friendly songs distinguished by pop-infused R&B. "The new songs are like big barroom fans that sweep the air around you when you dance," the magazine observed. "They make you want to roller skate. They're softer, more playful, almost approaching mirth. The lyrics have little to do with the blues—they're happier, more ethereal, like the 'rush of the wind' in 'Rock the Boat'" (July 1, 1974). ● Following the release of *Rockin' Soul* (1974), Karl Russell replaced Williams on lead vocals and kept The Hues Corporation on the disco chart with the title tracks to *Love Corporation* (1975) and their Warner Bros. debut *I Caught Your Act* (1976), yet the pop bliss of "Rock the Boat" remained their most essential contribution to the era.

GEORGE McCRAE

George McCrae realized he'd made it when he opened for James Brown at Madison Square Garden. That was July 4, 1974. Ten days later, "Rock Your Baby" topped the Hot 100 for two weeks, bringing a burst of Miami sunshine to the radio. ● "I was on top of the world," says McCrae. He became one of T.K. Records' marquee artists after signing with label president Henry Stone's Alston Productions five years earlier with his wife Gwen McCrae. The couple recorded as a duo and provided background vocals for Betty Wright, Timmy Thomas, and KC & the Sunshine Band, who featured McCrae's stratospheric wail on their single, "Queen of Clubs." ● KC used McCrae's voice to similar effect on "Rock Your Baby," the title track for McCrae's 1974 solo debut. "I was the only artist at T.K. Records at the time that had a high tenor type of voice," he says. "I did it in one take. I thought about my two favorite artists, Sam Cooke and Smokey Robinson. I put them in my mind. As I was singing 'Ahhh-hahhh, take me in your arms and rock me,' I thought about my favorite movie star when I was a kid—Tarzan!" ● "'Rock Your Baby' was released first in all the gay clubs," McCrae continues. "They broke it underground. Meanwhile, it was playing on R&B stations. The phone was ringing off the hook: 'Play that song again!' In the first week, Henry Stone had a back order of 50,000 copies in the Miami area alone." ● T.K. Records had one of its first solo stars as the "Sunshine Sound" spread across Europe with McCrae's follow-up singles "I Can't Leave You Alone," "I Ain't Lyin'," and "It's Been So Long," plus the Top 10 R&B smash "I Get Lifted." Indeed, McCrae's style of "Rock" kept on rollin' around the world.

THE MAIN INGREDIENT

"I'm going where the *fun* is." Sweet with just a hint of seduction, Main Ingredient lead vocalist Cuba Gooding invited listeners to untold pleasures on the trio's "Happiness is Just Around the Bend." He might as well have been singing about The Loft, where David Mancuso regularly spun the track for blissed-out revelers. ● Having already struck pop gold with "Everybody Plays the Fool," the six-minute track was The Main Ingredient's welcome overture to the clubs. "Exceptionally well done cut with strong string background, perfectly arranged spoken introduction and fine singing," *Billboard* exclaimed. Upon the single's release, RCA Records launched a summer-themed promotional campaign, "Happiness is Having a Ball with the Main Ingredient," in tandem with "Main Ingredient Week" during July 1974. ● "Looking at the heavy representation of rhythm and blues on the charts, you can't help coming away with the feeling that soul is today's pop music," noted Tom Draper (*Billboard* 1974), RCA's Director of Rhythm & Blues, speaking at the time about the label's success with New Birth, The Main Ingredient and The Hues Corporation, whose "Rock the Boat" brought a whole bunch of summer fun to the clubs and the airwaves. Group member Tony Silvester [pictured middle] found additional success in the clubs as co-producer with Bert DeCoteaux on tracks by Sister Sledge, Linda Lewis, Marlena Shaw, and Ben E. King's chart-topping "Supernatural Thing." ● The Main Ingredient continued to reach the clubs as "Rolling Down a Mountainside" and "Instant Love" circulated at New York discos like Leviticus and Adam's Apple. Motown signed Cuba Gooding in 1978 as the honey-voiced singer lent a song to the Motown-Casablanca film *Thank God It's Friday* (1978). Gooding always knew where fun could be found...

JAMES BROWN

"Music is still the master of the soul," James Brown once said. And the master of rhythm is still The Godfather of Soul. ● Throughout the 1970s, Brown [pictured with Lyn Collins in 1974] and his organization churned out slabs of combustible funk. "Get Up (I Feel Like Being a) Sex Machine" and "Give It Up or Turnit a Loose" were choice tracks at early New York clubs, especially Haven, Sanctuary, The Loft, and The Gallery, while Brown-produced albums like *Doing it to Death* (1973) by Fred Wesley & the J.B.'s, and vocalist Lyn Collins' *Think (About It)* (1972) were as indispensable to any discerning DJ as the singer's own releases. ● "I'm back!" Brown shouted on "Get Up Offa That Thing." His declaration was right on target. The song gave him a mid-decade smash in 1976. He later wrote in his autobiography: "The audience was sitting down, trying to do a sophisticated thing, *listening* to funk. One of the tightest bands they'd ever heard in their lives, and they were sitting. I had worked hard and dehydrated myself and was feeling depressed. I looked out at all those people sitting there, and because I was depressed, *they* looked depressed. I yelled, 'Get up offa that thing and dance til you feel better!' I probably meant until *I* felt better!" ● Three years later, Brown deemed himself "The Original Disco Man," which doubled as the title to his last album of the '70s. He even shot the album cover photo on the dance floor at midtown Manhattan's New York, New York discothèque. However, it was downtown at Paradise Garage where the album's "It's Too Funky in Here" became a club favorite. Disco was at its peak by then, but Brown never foreswore the funk.

JAMES BROWN

B.T. EXPRESS

"What's the hottest record in your club right now?" In November 1974, *Record World* columnist Vince Aletti had the definitive answer: "Express" by B.T. Express. Replete with train whistles, the track chugged to number one on *Billboard*'s newly formed "Disco Action" chart, where it reigned for five weeks during autumn 1974. ● The seven-piece B.T. Express crafted one scorching track after another on their debut album of the same year, *Do It ('Til You're Satisfied)*. Written by former Motown guitarist Billy Nichols, the title track had introduced the group's chunky blend of grooves earlier that year. The extended album version, mixed by disco master Tom Moulton, garnered substantial club play before topping the R&B chart and crossing over to the Hot 100, where it reached #2 and earned the group a gold single. ● Producer Jeff Lane continued working with the Brooklyn-based band, including their Top Five club hit "Peace Pipe" off *Non-Stop* (1975), plus Mandrill, Eddie Kendricks, and Brass Construction, who'd top *Record World*'s disco chart with "Movin'" for four weeks in 1976. However, Lane's success with B.T. Express reflected Scepter Records' pioneering approach towards promoting singles for the clubs. Mel Cheren, the label's Head of Production, made Scepter an early adopter of disco-formatted singles. ● "Scepter has been involved with discos for some time now," *Billboard* reported in November 1974. "Just recently, though, the label began releasing singles with a commercial, radio-oriented song on one side and a disco version on the flip. Cheren states that although a number of radio stations have time limitations on songs played, certain FM stations will go on the more lengthier disco version." Whether on the airwaves or in the discothèques, B.T. Express got everyone "satisfied."

JACKSON 5

The Jackson 5 brought a dash of disco flash to *The Tonight Show Starring Johnny Carson* in November 1974. "They're one of the most exciting groups in the entire world," Carson said. "They have sold over 50 million records. And this is their latest album, which is called *Dancing Machine* (1974)." ● An extended version of "Dancing Machine" had originally appeared on the group's *Get It Together* (1973) album and topped the R&B chart earlier that year. What most of Carson's viewing audience didn't know was that other tracks from the Jackson 5's two most recent albums were in heavy rotation at New York's hottest gay clubs, especially the marathon grooves of "Hum Along and Dance" and "I Am Love." ● "The Jackson 5 have been full of surprises the past few years," Vince Aletti noted in his column for *Record World* upon the release of the group's last Motown album, *Moving Violation* (1975). It opened with producer Brian Holland's thunderous remodeling of "Forever Came Today," originally recorded by Diana Ross & the Supremes. "The results are stunning," declared Aletti. "The cut everybody's talking about... Surely one of the finest productions this year." ● "Forever Came Today" topped *Record World*'s disco chart for four weeks during the summer of 1975, establishing Michael, Jermaine, Jackie, Marlon, Tito, and youngest brother Randy Jackson as princes in the expanding musical kingdom of disco. ● Signing with Epic Records, The Jacksons matured into a supergroup whose songs worked in clubs and arenas alike, capping the decade with two disco classics remixed by John Luongo from their album *Destiny* (1978), "Blame it on the Boogie" and "Shake Your Body (Down to the Ground)." Michael's command to "dance! shout!" on the latter cut foretold his own mantra for the dance floor: "Don't Stop 'Til You Get Enough."

HOT CHOCOLATE

Hot Chocolate had the recipe for disco heat—take a spicy groove, add a feverish lead vocal, and stir together for four minutes. That's exactly what the six-man band served on "You Sexy Thing" (1975). ● When lead vocalist Errol Brown [right] sang "I believe in miracles," it seemed like an entire lifetime had passed in the five years since their cover of John Lennon's "Give Peace a Chance" landed them a deal with Apple Records. With members hailing from Jamaica, Trinidad, England, Grenada, and The Bahamas, Hot Chocolate mixed together a variety of musical influences that distinguished them from other pop and rock bands of the era. The London-based group were ready for the clubs. ● "It never bothered me that we were known as a disco band because I was a disco person," Brown told *The Independent* years later. "Before I was married, I was in nightclubs all the time and would get home at four in the morning." Brown drew from experience in writing the group's "Disco Queen" on their debut album *Cicero Park* (1974). "Disco Queen" was among the singles that launched Atlantic Records' "Disco Disc" Series in May 1975, a specially curated campaign that furnished discothèques with non-commercial singles for club play. ● In July 1979, *The New York Times* hailed Hot Chocolate's fascinating jaunt across the 1970s pop landscape, culminating with *Going Through the Motions*: "The new album confirms Errol Brown and company's really wonderful blend of danceable basics and fresh ideas," critic John Rockwell wrote. "This is a disco record with a pulsing beat and a twanging bass line. But the sheer *sound* of this disk, with its airy textures and unusual instrumental colorations, makes it worth buying. Add to that Mr. Brown's distinctively hysterical vocals and wicked sense of humor and you have a record to cherish." The recipe worked every time.

OHIO PLAYERS

Stevie Wonder immediately knew the Ohio Players had a hit when he heard "Fire." "We were staying at his hotel on Sunset Boulevard," recalls drummer James "Diamond" Williams. "Stevie was staying next door to me. I played him the rhythm track to 'Fire.' It had so much smoke and energy to it. He said it was so hot, we could name it 'Fire.' Stevie actually gave us the name and then we developed the words and the horns." ● The vocal interplay between Leroy "Sugarfoot" Bonner (guitar) and Billie Beck (keyboards) stoked a musical inferno and powered "Fire" to number one on the pop and R&B charts. "When I first got in the band, I really didn't know what a hit record was," Diamond says. "I'd never crossed the country, listening to the radio, to hear a song that was being played every hour-and-a-half! Is *that* what a hit record is?" ● "Fire" also exploded in the clubs and would join the group's second number one pop hit, "Love Rollercoaster," on *Record World*'s "Essential Disco Singles of 1975" list. "How much more fun can you have than being on a rollercoaster?" says Diamond, who sang falsetto with Beck. "It was just that idea of creating something, musically, that everybody could relate to. You even know from the rhythm that I put 'Rollercoaster' in, it's got that herky jerky thing, but it's not a funk track. It's happy-go-lucky pop." ● Ohio Players became a million-selling group with "Fire" and "Love Rollercoaster" while their chart-topping albums—*Skin Tight* (1974), *Fire* (1974), *Honey* (1975)—set a new precedent: Ohio Players became the first Black band in history to write and produce three consecutive platinum albums.

OHIO PLAYERS

AL DOWNING & DON DOWNING

Al Downing and Don Downing led innovations that forever changed dance music. "I met Don Downing [seated] when I was working at Media Sound in New York," recalls producer Tony Bongiovi. "He called me. He had heard about me and told me he was a songwriter and a singer. He lived in DC, so I went there to meet him. I met Don and his brother Al and some other writers and musicians." ● After Bongiovi, Meco Monardo, and Jay Ellis produced "Dream World" for Don Downing, Scepter Records' Head of Production Mel Cheren gave Tom Moulton an extra copy of the master. "I encouraged Tom to take it home and experiment with it on his own," Cheren recalled in his autobiography. "Tom stripped the song to the bare percussion tracks, eliminated all singing and musical instruments until what he had left was a sort of tribal pounding that went on and on, perfect for dancing yourself into a trance. Right there, on his very first time in the studio, not only had he remixed a song into a classic, he had also invented a standard that would sweep the record industry almost overnight—the disco break—in which the music stops but the beat goes on." Produced and engineered by Tony Bongiovi, the four-minute and 20-second "Disco Mix" of "Dream World" was released in November 1974, selling 10,000 copies within a matter of days, all without radio play. ● Moulton pioneered yet another invention with Bongiovi, Monardo and Ellis' production of "I'll Be Holding On" by Al Downing [standing] on Chess Records. Moulton had finished his mix of "I'll Be Holding On" but the studio had run out of seven-inch acetates, typically used for reference singles. Media Sound mastering engineer José Rodriguez instead pressed the track on 12-inch vinyl. By mere necessity, Moulton discovered that 12-inch vinyl offered a more robust sound for singles geared towards club play and a new industry standard was born. ● When "I'll Be Holding On" topped the disco chart in December 1974, Al Downing had two reasons to celebrate: a number one hit and the birth of the 12-inch single.

GLORIA GAYNOR

Le Jardin staged a historic coronation on March 3, 1975, when the National Association of Discothèque Disk Jockeys crowned Gloria Gaynor "Queen of the Discothèques." ● The title was well-earned. Two months earlier, Gaynor's debut *Never Can Say Goodbye* (1975) unveiled the first non-stop "disco suite" mixed by Tom Moulton as "Honeybee," "Never Can Say Goodbye," and "Reach Out, I'll Be There" stirred dancers into an 18-minute frenzy. "Tom's idea of blending the songs was great," says Gaynor. "Three or four minutes of a single was never long enough for me. I loved how he incorporated the beat in a way that really inspired dancing. You didn't get tired for some reason. ● "I know exactly when I first met with Tom. I met Tom right after I recorded 'Never Can Say Goodbye.' I was in my manager's office. My manager's desk faced the door, and I was facing the desk. When Tom came in, my manager lifted his arm and beckoned Tom to come in. I turned around and when Tom saw that it was me, he fell on his knees and started bowing! [laughs] I'll never forget it." ● Even before the album's release, "Never Can Say Goodbye" had become the first recording to top *Billboard*'s "Disco Action" chart, published on October 26, 1974. Gaynor would return to number one a year later with "Casanova Brown," "(If You Want It) Do It Yourself," and "How High the Moon," bringing a combination of sass and sophistication to the clubs. "The music sounds very expensive," says Moulton. "The thing about Gloria was 'New York'—the glitz, the glamour. It's razzmatazz, bright lights. You're not going to sing these songs in jeans." ● Gaynor ultimately closed the decade with a timeless anthem: "I Will Survive." Produced by Freddie Perren on the singer's *Love Tracks* (1978) album, the song topped the Hot 100 and became the first, and only, record to win a GRAMMY Award for Best Disco Recording. Gloria Gaynor not only survived; she soared.

7

BOHANNON

Hamilton Bohannon got the party going on *Soul Train*, especially as dancers grooved along to "South African Man," the hypnotizing hit from his second album *Keep on Dancin'* (1974). Months later, Bohannon appeared on *Top of the Pops*, celebrating the international success of "Disco Stomp," the playful but no less soulful groove that reached the UK Top 10 and, along with "Foot Stompin' Music," made his third LP *Insides Out* (1975) one of *Record World*'s "Essential Disco Albums of 1975." ● A former band leader and arranger for the Motortown Revue, where he'd backed Motown's top acts including Marvin Gaye, The Temptations, and Stevie Wonder, Bohannon was an early pioneer of a sound that extended well beyond the disco era. In fact, "Disco Stomp" was a source of inspiration for guitarist Johnny Marr on The Smiths' "How Soon is Now?" while blockbuster acts like Jay-Z and Justin Timberlake would later search Bohannon's albums for samples. ● "The thing about Bohannon's musical style that influenced us were his relentlessly driving rhythms, four to the bar, performed by his entire rhythm section on guitar, bass, drums and percussion," recalled Talking Heads drummer Chris Frantz in *The New York Times*. "While Bohannon's approach to music was easy and fun to dance to, his production values were not overly slick and polished... There was something very visceral about his songs." ● "This album is dedicated to all my Disco friends," Bohannon wrote on *Summertime Groove* (1978). On his third LP for Mercury Records, he propelled those friends to stratospheric heights with "Let's Start the Dance," a Top 10 club hit that spotlighted Carolyn Crawford's incendiary vocals. "Don't you wanna dance?" she screamed over Bohannon's relentless rhythms. It was more of a statement than a question... and everyone on the dance floor was quick to obey her command.

THE SPINNERS

"The rhythm and the drums are the heartbeat," Thom Bell once said. Bell brought a special kind of heartbeat to the albums he produced for the Spinners, resuscitating the former Motown act's career with a trio of gold-selling singles on Atlantic Records, "One of a Kind (Love Affair)," "Could It Be I'm Falling in Love," and "I'll Be Around." ● "Someone dared me to write a three-chord song," Bell noted about the latter tune, his first hit production for the Spinners in 1972. "'Tommy Bell, you always write all these hard little intricate things. I bet you can't write a three-chord song.' Okay, I'll try. That's how 'I'll Be Around' came about. The same three chords over and over again." Bell invited Philadelphia International songwriter Phil Hurtt to write the lyrics and put Spinners vocalist Bobby Smith [second from left] on lead vocal. "I heard Bobby's voice. 'Oh my goodness *that's* the voice, man,'" he said. "It sent chills up my spine." ● Bell also shone the spotlight on Philippé Wynne [center] for songs like "The Rubberband Man" (1976). "I've worked with some of the best and no one could out-sing Philippé," Bell said. "He sang best with an audience of his peers. All the artists wanted to know when Philippé would be in the studio. They'd make their vacation time around the time The Spinners were in the studio. Who would be in the studio? Pendergrass, Eddie Levert, Lou Rawls, The Three Degrees, Sister Sledge... the whole crew!" ● As the decade progressed, vocalist John Edwards replaced Wynne while producer Michael Zager reoriented their sound on *Dancin' and Lovin'* (1979). From a cover photo shot at Xenon to the group's rendition of The Four Seasons' "Working My Way Back to You," the album spun the Spinners into a shiny whirl of pop-disco opulence.

EARTH, WIND & FIRE

"How can you explain inspiration? Put together the right musicians and if the timing is right–it just comes through," Earth, Wind & Fire founder Maurice White once said. ● In 1975, the timing was perfect for Earth, Wind & Fire. *That's the Way of the World* (1975) topped the pop and R&B album charts, while "Shining Star" duplicated the triumph on the single charts and gave EWF their first of several GRAMMY Awards. *Record World* named it one of "The Most Essential Disco Albums" of 1975, with songs like "Happy Feelin'" and "Africano" finding a home in the clubs. *Gratitude* (1975) and *Spirit* (1976) spawned even more infectious hits, with "Sing A Song," "Getaway," and "Saturday Nite" amplifying the group's appeal in the discos and on the airwaves. ● Attired in glittering stage costumes by Bill Whitten, their concerts were among the most theatrical shows of the era. "The *All 'n All* show put us on the map in terms of live stuff," says bassist Verdine White. "It was an incredible time." "Fantasy," one of the key tracks on *All 'n All*, resonated with the escapist spirit of the clubs. "'Fantasy' came out around the same time that *Star Wars* (1977) came out," says Verdine, who wrote the track with Maurice and Eddie Del Barrio. "The lyric was sort of similar." ● After taking "a ride in the sky," EWF brought listeners to "Boogie Wonderland" on *I Am* (1979). The band's GRAMMY-winning duet with The Emotions was co-written by Allee Willis, who'd collaborated on what became EWF's signature hit, "September." "'Boogie Wonderland' was a new direction for us, to record a tune that was strictly for dancing without any spiritual overtones involved," Maurice noted. "The momentum from our previous hits was reiterated in the energy of the rhythm and upbeat lyrics." Beyond the dance floor, the music of Earth, Wind & Fire made everyone feel like a shining star.

LABELLE

Labelle personified all that was fierce and fabulous. In music and style, [left to right] Nona Hendryx, Sarah Dash, and Patti LaBelle fashioned their own sensibility. Wearing space-themed costumes designed by Larry LeGaspi, their theatricality attracted listeners who defied convention. ● "We brought people together from all different walks of life to one place," says Nona Hendryx, recalling Labelle's historic performance in 1974 as the first Black female group to perform at the Metropolitan Opera House. "A great group of New Yorkers came out, from Salvador Dalí to the people who had supported us from Patti LaBelle & the Bluebelles days. That was a big deal for us." ● The trio's recording of "Lady Marmalade" was a club sensation everywhere from Studio One in West Hollywood to Better Days in Manhattan. Four Seasons songwriter Bob Crewe had offered the song to Labelle and manager Vicki Wickham for their session with producer Allen Toussaint in New Orleans. "We had no idea what he was talking about because none of us spoke French," Hendryx recalls. "'Voulez-vous couchez avec moi, çe soir?'—that sounds hot! We like that one!" ● Their instincts rewarded them with gold records for "Lady Marmalade" and their album *Nightbirds* (1974). After topping the pop and R&B charts, Labelle appeared on *The Cher Show*, where the host joined them for their latest club hit, "What Can I Do For You?," a song that more closely reflected the spirt of the trio. "'Lady Marmalade' was kind of like a door opener, in a way, for what we really wanted to say," says Hendryx. ● Labelle's next albums, *Phoenix* (1975) and *Chameleon* (1976), appealed to the clubs while continuing to spotlight the trio's power as vocalists, songwriters, and performers before they each ventured solo in 1977. To quote Sarah Dash, "Our group was an unchallenged musical entity."

BETTY WRIGHT

An eruption of combustible Miami soul hit New York during the winter of 1975. It even seemed to make the walls sweat at clubs like 12 West and Flamingo. It was "Where is the Love?" by Betty Wright. ● Soaring to number two on the disco chart, it was also the latest smash by a singer who'd amassed half a dozen R&B hits as a teenager, including "Clean Up Woman," which earned Wright a gold record and a GRAMMY nomination. She'd become a best-selling solo artist at T.K. Records, the Hialeah-based record company that distributed several independent labels and would become a gold mine of disco hits throughout the 1970s. ● "The T.K. sound is a combination of Latin, blues, Caribbean—a whole mixture of music down here in Miami," said T.K. founder Henry Stone. "You can feel it in the rhythms of the records." Or, as Betty Wright explained, "It's R&B dipped with a little Salsa. It's just got a little hot sauce on it." ● That sound is the foundation of *Danger High Voltage* (1974), Wright's third album for Stone's Alston label. It featured several of T.K.'s core musicians, including Timmy Thomas, Latimore, Little Beaver, Clarence Reid, and members of KC & the Sunshine Band. In fact, Sunshine Band founder Harry Wayne Casey co-produced and co-wrote "Where is the Love?," which won the GRAMMY for "Best R&B Song," a victory Wright shared with Casey and Richard Finch. ● A few years after "Where is the Love?" and a cover of Allen Toussaint's "Shoorah! Shoorah!" gave Wright a pair of Top 40 UK hits, she appeared on another T.K. classic that would define the era, "Dance With Me" by Peter Brown. Her "high voltage" style contoured every note.

RUFUS & CHAKA KHAN

Rufus & Chaka Khan knew how to start a record. The introduction to "Once You Get Started" was like a rocket launching into space, with Chaka's voice furnishing a fiery source of fuel. That kind of fanfare thrilled the crowd at Le Jardin in New York City where DJ Bobby Guttadaro made it a regular part of his set. ● "'Once You Get Started' was written by Gavin Christopher, myself, and Tony Maiden [second from right] in a basement in Chicago in '72," says Rufus bassist Bobby Watson [left]. "We kept the song in our head until we joined Rufus and began to record *Rufusized* (1974). We needed songs and this was a good one, tempo-wise, with a decent hook." ● The five-piece band bridged funk-rock with the discothèques, even covering "Jive Talkin'" shortly after the Bee Gees' original topped the pop charts in 1975. When drummer Hawk Wolinski joined Rufus, the band's albums brimmed with even more original material, especially on *Masterjam* (1979) produced by Quincy Jones. "Any Love," which surveyed the social rituals of the era, and "Do You Love What You Feel" both made the Top 5 on the disco chart, underscoring the band's staying power in the clubs. ● "When we played 'Do You Love What You Feel' in the recording studio for Quincy, he thought it was horrible, so we went back to the drawing board—rehearsing," Watson recalls. "We played that song 100 times in a row over a three-day time period. By the time the third day ended, it was soooooo tight. Hawk then brought in 'Any Love,' which we played a bunch of times until it felt good to us. Loved the bouncy groove between the bass and drums!" Indeed, Rufus grooved to perfection in the key of Q.

THE BLACKBYRDS

The Blackbyrds were a refreshing tonic for the discos. When trumpet master and professor Donald Byrd brought his students together at Howard University, he could hardly forecast how the band's fusion of jazz and R&B would take off in discothèques. ● As the Blackbyrds balanced classroom studies with touring commitments, "Walking in Rhythm," a breezy and buoyant track from their second album *Flying Start* (1974), glided into the clubs. "It was about what it *said,"* notes drummer Keith Killgo [second from left]. "It was about Joe Hall playing that bass line. It was about all the crescendos, glissandos, arpeggios, and diatonic scales that Kevin Toney was playing. It was about the bossa nova beat that I played." ● DJs scoured The Blackbyrds' first two albums for tracks like "Gut Level" while the band built on the GRAMMY-nominated success of "Walking in Rhythm" with *City Life* (1975), an album that spawned a bona-fide classic, "Rock Creek Park." The band hatched the groove during a soundcheck in Camden, New Jersey. "We were opening for The Commodores," Killgo recalls. "We just started jamming. We had these little Marantz Superscope tape recorders. When we got done with the gig, we played it for Byrd. He said, 'We're going to record that.' We flew back to LA When we were listening to the playback, I just started singing, 'Doing it in the park, doing it after dark, oh yeah.' I didn't write a word of it down!" ● Killgo's spontaneous wordplay became an anthem for the famed park in Washington, DC "You could go to Rock Creek Park and get off of the wheel," he adds. "It brought some kind of peace within a city that's bustling." And in the clubs, "Rock Creek Park" furnished a timeless hook for the dance floor.

SILVER CONVENTION

Silver Convention introduced a constellation of vocalists and musicians that turned Munich into the main hub of Eurodisco. "I was very much influenced by R&B music, Barry White and Isaac Hayes," says Hungarian songwriter and arranger Sylvester Levay, whose nickname "Silver" inspired the group's moniker. "We were very much hooked on the Philadelphia sound. That was this really great groove with the hi-hat." ● Recorded in 1974, "Save Me" introduced the Silver Convention template—Levay's crisply arranged strings, soaring above drummer Keith Forsey and bassist Gary Unwin's bed of rhythm. "'Save Me' really did represent a new sound," says Lucy Neale, who sang the lyrics alongside Munich-based session singers Gitta Walther, Roberta Kelly, and Betsy Allen. "There were these classical musicians from the Bavarian Symphony Orchestra playing in the studio on this disco tune! It was really exciting." ● Midland International Records acquired "Save Me" for North America in February 1975, building on the label's previous club success with "Doctor's Orders" by Carol Douglas, and requested a full-length album. The same set of musicians and vocalists, plus Jackie Carter, reconvened at Union Studio in Munich to record what became *Record World*'s #1 "Most Essential Disco Album of 1975." It also spawned a GRAMMY Award-winning smash that topped the pop, R&B, *and* disco charts—"Fly, Robin, Fly." ● Producer Michael Kunze hired [from left to right] Linda G. Thompson, Ramona Wulf, and "Lady Bump" vocalist Penny McLean for promotional appearances, though the trio wouldn't record together until Silver Convention's second album, *Get Up and Boogie* (1976). A series of lineup changes led to the group's final Top 10 disco hit "Spend the Night With Me" (1978), but their impact far exceeded their four-year lifespan. ● Because of Silver Convention, Eurodisco was now in full flight.

APPLY:
AGENT
25

54
54

1976–1977

"I'll let in anyone who looks like they'll make things fun." Steve Rubell is guiding a *New York Times* reporter through Studio 54 as resident DJ Richie Kaczor dazzles the crowd with records by CHIC, Odyssey, and T-Connection. "Disco, that's where the happy people go," The Trammps sing as dancers spin and twirl underneath tubes of flashing lights. Seven months since Rubell and co-owner Ian Schrager opened Studio 54 in April 1977 and it has already welcomed untold numbers of "happy people"... those lucky enough to pass through the doors.

"We were part of the chosen few," says André De Shields, who immortalized the title role in *The Wiz* on Broadway at the time. "We could show up at Studio 54 and the doorman at the velvet stanchion would look over everyone and point to us from *The Wiz* to come in, that kind of thing." As the lead vocalist in the GRAMMY-nominated Dr. Buzzard's Original Savannah Band, whose debut modernized big-band sophistication for the discothèques, Cory Daye had carte blanche in the club. "The energy was like a New Year's Eve party every night," she says. "I would go up to the mezzanine and watch the mechanical light pillars go up and down, metallic confetti falling from the ceiling, the spoon and the moon. I was so fascinated and enamored by it.

"When a certain song came on, the people would just rush to the dance floor. There was no contact dancing—the hustle was pretty much on its way out—but it was just an amazing experience to see all the cultures together. It was a fusion of cultures, which described my life and my band, so I was right at home there."

"Studio 54 was the place," adds Linda Clifford. "Crazy parties. If you could think it, you would see it. It was like a circus. Just an amazing place to be. I worked 54 so many times. It was like a second home to me. The people there treated me so well. The crowd always seemed to enjoy my show. I always had a good time with them. That was the most important thing: making sure that they had fun."

Well before Studio 54 opened, disco had become a business juggernaut. "A four-billion-dollar market and still growing," *Billboard* announced in February 1977, with dance music offering more variety than ever. "There is no longer a single, readily identifiable disco beat, but a kaleidoscope of sounds that are melodic and danceable," Tom Moulton told the magazine. In the clubs, records by veteran artists like Stevie Wonder and the Bee Gees were mixed in with a range of new acts like Grace Jones, Boney M., and The Ritchie Family, while everyone from ABBA to Marvin Gaye scored number one pop hits with songs that had club-centric storylines.

Beyond the charts, disco itself remained as idiosyncratic as ever, especially on several productions by Laurin Rinder and W. Michael Lewis, whose studio creations, El Coco ("Let's Get It Together," "Cocomotion") and Le Pamplemousse ("Le Spank"), joined their own "Lust" from *Seven Deadly Sins* (1977) among the most tantalizing releases on AVI Records. Rinder & Lewis also produced acts for the newly hatched Butterfly Records in Los Angeles, where Saint Tropez ("On a Rien à Perdre") and Tuxedo Junction ("Moonlight Serenade") reflected the duo's high-gloss sound, spanning everything from European sophistication to a more literal translation of the '40s sensibilities popularized by Dr. Buzzard's Original Savannah Band.

12-inch singles had also grown as the preferred format to approximate the club music experience at home. Nearly a year after Atlantic Records introduced its series of promotional 12-inch singles for DJs, New York-based Salsoul Records released the industry's first commercially available 12-inch single, "Ten Percent" by Double Exposure, in May 1976. A year later, T.K. Records was the first label to certify a gold record for a 12-inch single when Peter Brown's "Do You Wanna Get Funky With Me" tallied one million sales.

Donna Summer continued to reflect disco's penchant for musical and conceptual innovation on albums like *Four Seasons of Love* (1976) and the two-LP *Once Upon a Time* (1977). André De Shields recalls, "When Donna Summer would come on in the disco, you knew it was approaching the time for the ceiling to open and the six-foot disco ball would come down, and you've saved a hit of cocaine for that purpose, so that the world, the universe, the cosmos would *expand* for you and you would dance yourself into another *dimension*."

Summer and producers Giorgio Moroder and Pete Bellotte transported dancers to a cosmic paradise on "I Feel Love," a pulsating production that closed *I Remember Yesterday* (1977), the singer's homage to popular music's past, present, and future. "When we got to the last track, which was to be the future, we had to sit down and think, *What can we do here?*" Bellotte explains. "We'd used small Moogs [modular synthesizers] before. Kraftwerk were around and there was a lot of classical electronic stuff going on, as well. In Munich, there was a classical musician Eberhard Schoener. He owned the Moog IIIP, which he hired out. His programmer, Robbie Wedel, brought these three pieces [comprising the synthesizer] along to the studio. He set them up. The only thing that we added on there afterwards was a real bass drum. Otherwise, it's all synths.

"When we recorded Donna, she immediately sang it in head voice, which we hadn't told her to do. It was the juxtaposition of this lilting head voice above this relentless pace that added so much magic to 'I Feel Love.'"

"I Feel Love" revealed a new frontier in disco. "It was one of those records that pushed the form along," says Vince Aletti. "Kraftwerk kind of opened the way but in a much more limited audience. Donna and Giorgio pushed that to a much larger audience. It was really a new thing for her and a way for people to appreciate what exactly it was that Giorgio did because, not long after that, he did *From Here to Eternity* (1977), which was a great electronic record." Moroder's progressive approach to music would also shape his Oscar-winning score to *Midnight Express* (1978), produced by Casablanca's Filmworks division.

At the time, *Billboard* named Casablanca Records the industry's number one disco label, a position it held over four consecutive years between 1977 and 1980. Label founder and president Neil Bogart presided like a ringmaster. "Neil was a maverick and he was very much a Renaissance man," Summer recalled years later. "He was someone that could take your idea to the next 700 levels in about 40 seconds. He could take a lot of foreign objects and make them work together. He was like a magnetic comet moving through a sphere of space, attaching and drawing everything to himself that came near him."

In 1977 alone, Casablanca's roster of artists could power an entire night of dancing. Donna Summer, Giorgio Moroder, Santa Esmeralda, Munich Machine, Roberta Kelly, Pattie Brooks, Love & Kisses, Meco Monardo, whose "Star Wars Theme/Cantina Band" (a disco rendition of the epic movie theme) gave Casablanca its first number one pop hit, plus funk bands like Parliament and Cameo, all furnished DJs with dazzling cuts everywhere from Studio One in West Hollywood to Le Dome in Acapulco to Baia Degli Angeli on the Adriatic coast of Italy.

And Casablanca's next signing would introduce one of the era's most successful acts—Village People. Produced by Jacques Morali, *Village People* (1977) toured different enclaves where gay men experienced a newfound sense of liberation, "San Francisco (You've Got Me)," "In Hollywood (Everybody is a Star)," "Fire Island," and "Village People" (named for Greenwich Village). "Jacques sold it to Neil Bogart as a concept album," says Felipe Rose, the group's original Native American who'd inspired Morali's idea for Village People when Morali saw him dance at the Anvil in New York's Meatpacking District. "When Neil heard the first album, he loved it. It was Neil who pushed and said, 'We need a group that can support these four songs.'"

Village People topped the disco chart for seven consecutive weeks during September and October 1977, beginning their reign as a pop culture phenomenon. Just a few weeks before New Year's Eve, however, disco would skyrocket to a whole other stratosphere with just three words: *Saturday Night Fever.*

THE TRAMMPS

"Memphis got its sound. Motown got its sound. I'm gonna create my own sound," says Earl Young, founder of The Trammps and drummer for MFSB, the orchestra behind countless hits recorded at Philadelphia's Sigma Sound Studios. "I created my four-on-the-floor bass drum beat and my hi hat," Young continues. "When disco came out, they said 'Earl's a disco drummer' but that was actually the way that I played, automatically." ● Young's style had a permanent place in The Trammps. He formed the group with Baker-Harris-Young (BHY), the production company he created with guitarist Norman Harris and bassist Ronnie Baker. "I wanted a name that nobody would ever forget," says Young [seated left, with Harold Wade, Jimmy Ellis, Stan Wade, Robert Upchurch]. "I couldn't use 'The Tramps' because there was a rock group called Supertramp. I put another 'm' in the name. That's why The Trammps is spelled with two m's." ● "Zing Went the Strings of My Heart" (1972) launched The Trammps' career on Buddah Records and BHY's Golden Fleece before they signed with Atlantic. "That's Where the Happy People Go" and "Disco Party" topped the disco chart for seven weeks in spring 1976, while the title track to *Disco Inferno* (1977) brought them back to number one. "Disco Inferno" was only a modest pop hit, however, until a certain movie came along. ● "They wanted to put *Saturday Night Fever* out and they needed another song," Young recalls. "I said, 'We got a song called 'Disco Inferno.' It was out earlier but it wasn't a big hit.' It was the last song to go into *Saturday Night Fever*. Wherever the movie went, we went!" Atlantic re-released "Disco Inferno" in 1978. This time, it exploded across radio, television, and movies, and became *the* defining anthem for the disco era.

KC & THE SUNSHINE BAND

In a March 1976 feature about T.K. Records, *The New York Times* applauded KC & the Sunshine Band, saying: "They are one of the most exciting groups performing today... On stage, KC becomes truly possessed by his rhythms, happily rocking from side to side as he stands hunched over his electric piano, skipping across the floor, proselytizing his listeners to give in to the spirit of his fervent sound." ● Band founder, songwriter and producer, Harry Wayne Casey ("KC"), had already written songs for T.K.'s family of artists, including Betty Wright, Clarence Reid, and Timmy Thomas, before launching his own band with the Top 40 R&B hit "Blow Your Whistle" (1973). "We called the band the 'Sunshine Junkanoo Band' at first," he recalled, speaking to the GRAMMY Awards website. "Junkanoo is from the Bahamas and uses a lot of steel drums, horns, whistles, and cowbells. It's an intensely percussion-infused sound and it takes over your body when you're around it." ● "KC's music is body music," *The New York Times* added. "On the discothèque circuit, every year, without fail, there is one joyful pop song which becomes a rhythmic refrain for summer in the city. The summer of '74 that tune was 'Rock Your Baby'—written and produced by KC and partner Richard Finch for singer George McCrae. This past summer's disco anthem was 'Get Down Tonight.'" ● It was the latter tune that sparked KC & the Sunshine Band's string of chart-topping pop hits from 1975–1977 that continued with "That's the Way (I Like It)," "(Shake, Shake, Shake) Shake Your Booty," "I'm Your Boogie Man," and the number one R&B smash "Keep It Comin' Love," plus the high-profile placement of "Boogie Shoes" on the *Saturday Night Fever* (1977) soundtrack. With KC piloting the grooves, the sound of sunshine was painted in platinum.

Rhodes

CAROL DOUGLAS

When Studio 54 opened its doors in April 1977, Carol Douglas was among the first of the era's disco queens to perform at the club. It was during another occasion at the club, however, where she met a fan of her hit "Doctor's Orders"—Diana Ross. As Douglas told *The Montreal Gazette* in 2013, "I was invited to Burt Reynolds' birthday party and she said, 'I just love 'Doctor's Orders.' I told her 'Hey, do you want it? You can have it!'" ● Douglas had helped bridge the emerging discothèque sound in the clubs with Top 40 radio when "Doctor's Orders" began its ascent in November 1974. It was only the third single released by RCA-distributed Midland International Records but followed a similar pattern to RCA's success with The Hues Corporation's "Rock the Boat" earlier that year. "'Skyrocketing' is the word for what's happening with this happy disco-perfect single," *Billboard* reported at the time. "It sold 100,000 in its first week of release, with rack-jobbers placing heavy orders even before it crossed over from the soul chart to the Hot 100." ● The Brooklyn-born vocalist took success in stride as "Doctor's Orders" climbed to number two on the disco chart and gave her a Top 20 pop and R&B hit. She recalled, "The first time I heard 'Doctor's Orders' on the radio, I was making lunch for my kids and they said, 'Hey Mom! Mom! It's your song!' And there it was. The kids were jumping up and down and, I have to admit, I was pretty excited too." ● Before they formed CHIC, Nile Rodgers and Bernard Edwards' Big Apple Band toured with Douglas in Italy. A year later, she topped the disco chart with "Midnight Love Affair" and subsequently recorded her own versions of ABBA's "Dancing Queen" and the Bee Gees' "Night Fever." In fact, "Carol Douglas" graced the marquee outside 2001 Odyssey in *Saturday Night Fever,* a fitting gesture for an artist who'd popularized disco from the very beginning.

CROWN HEIGHTS AFFAIR

Well before Brooklyn was synonymous with *Saturday Night Fever*, it spawned a cadre of bands whose sound defined the formative years of disco, including B.T. Express, Brass Construction, and Crown Heights Affair. The latter group topped *Record World*'s disco chart in July 1975 with "Dreaming a Dream," a sweeping instrumental track that doubled as the title of their debut album for De-Lite Records, home to Kool & the Gang. "It was a burst of excitement and sexuality," says William Anderson, the group's leader and guitarist [seated fourth from left]. "It was just a whole new sound." ● Crown Heights Affair quickly returned to the disco chart with "Every Beat of My Heart," a rousing, horn-driven track arranged by Meco Monardo that peaked at number two, and "Dancin'," a Top 10 hit from their second De-Lite album, *Do It Your Way* (1976). "What inspired me to do 'Dancin'' was a song from Isaac Hayes," says Anderson, who conceived the track's smoldering pulse. "I took the idea from *Shaft*. That was in my DNA. I used to love anything that Isaac did." ● As the decade progressed, Crown Heights Affair achieved success in the UK with hits like "Galaxy of Love" and "You Gave Me Love" while finding a second home in New York at Paradise Garage, one of the city's most influential clubs. "Paradise Garage was our home base," says Anderson. "We must have played at the Garage three times a year. The DJs were outstanding. They loved us like brothers. They opened up their hearts. I was a night owl. I would get there around 1:00 a.m. and I would stay until 10 the next morning. ● "I ain't never seen a club like it."

ANDREA TRUE CONNECTION

"How do you like it?" The question wafted breezily through discothèques and onto radio where Andrea True Connection's gold-selling "More, More, More" spawned one of the most seductive hooks of 1976. ● Long before Andrea True cooed the lyrics, Gregg Diamond and Godfrey Diamond had written the song for a movie their older brother Jack Doroshow—also known as groundbreaking drag performer Flawless Sabrina—was working on. As an engineer at New York's Media Sound Studios, Godfrey had mixed albums by Kool & the Gang and Crown Heights Affair, which influenced his approach to the song's rhythm. "We used to rehearse it every day," he says. "I'm playing drums and Gregg is on a Spinet piano. We were coming up with ideas all the time—all dance, real straight up four-on-the-floor." ● Though the movie flopped, Gregg and Godfrey brought "More, More, More" down to Federal Records in Jamaica where Andrea True had just completed a film project. "We got those amazing horn players," says Godfrey. "I put on some cowbell down there. We rehearsed Andrea really well. I was able to dupe [duplicate] her a whole bunch of times and put in all these harmonizers and digital delays. Then I put it all on a sampler, so there's like 10 of her. That's why it's so breathy." ● DJs began adding "More, More, More" to their repertoire in January 1976. Months later, the Diamond brothers wrote and produced an accompanying LP, which *Record World* called a "surprisingly substantial and attractive album." Though Andrea True would burnish her disco crown by name-checking New York haunts Regine's, 12 West, and the Barefoot Boy on another Top 40 Diamond production, "N.Y., You Got Me Dancing," and working with producer Michael Zager on *White Witch* (1977), "More, More, More" would always be the song that got the "action going"...

VICKI SUE ROBINSON

On any given night during March 1976, Vicki Sue Robinson's latest single could transform dance floors into red-hot infernos. Her kinetic vocal performance on "Turn the Beat Around" invigorated New York crowds everywhere from Flamingo in Soho to the upper west side's Continental Baths. Written by Peter Jackson and Gerald Jackson from the Philadelphia-based vocal quartet A Touch of Class, and produced by RCA VP Warren Schatz, "Turn the Beat Around" heralded the arrival of a dynamic new artist. ● In reviewing "Turn the Beat Around," *Record World* applauded the "extraordinary, driven vocal by Vicki Sue Robinson that makes use of her voice as another instrument." Nine months later, *Billboard* named her Most Promising New Disco Artist (October 9, 1976). The Harlem-born singer, who'd performed in Broadway productions of *Hair* and *Jesus Christ Superstar,* was surprised by her newfound role as a disco queen. "I was just a wide-eyed kid when I recorded 'Turn the Beat Around,'" she later told *Billboard.* "At the time, I was heavily into theater, jazz, and Steely Dan." ● "Turn the Beat Around" topped the disco chart for four weeks in the spring of 1976 and soared to number 10 on the Hot 100. It even earned Robinson a GRAMMY nomination for "Best Pop Vocal Performance, Female." Throughout the '70s, her four albums on RCA showcased how her vivacious approach adapted to ballads and rock-tinged funk as much as disco favorites like "Daylight," "Hold Tight," "Trust in Me," and "Nighttime Fantasy" from the 1979 film *Nocturna.* ● Robinson continued to record dance singles through the 1980s and 1990s, and staged a series of one-woman shows, before passing away in 2000. *The New York Times* remembered her as "a powerful, exuberant belter." And disco didn't get more exuberant than "Turn the Beat Around."

VAN McCOY

Washington DC celebrated "Van McCoy Day" on April 27, 1976. McCoy's musical achievements as an artist, songwriter, arranger, and producer were added to the Congressional Record. That included several hundred credits and one game-changing single—"The Hustle." ● A year earlier, "The Hustle" further kindled a dance phenomenon that McCoy had only recently experienced firsthand. "When I wrote 'The Hustle,' I had never seen the dance," he shared with Maryland Public Television. "I went to a couple of clubs in New York and saw the dance actually being done. My first reaction to the dance was, it was a combination of the old jitterbug and some of the Latin dances like the tango and also the merengue. It was a touch dance." ● Recorded with McCoy's Soul City Symphony, "The Hustle" topped the pop and R&B charts while *Record World* deemed him "Dance Master for 1975" with *Disco Baby* (1975) and *The Disco Kid* (1975), plus his chart-topping productions for Faith, Hope & Charity ("To Each His Own") and David Ruffin ("Walk Away from Love"). Both acts would also record one of McCoy's greatest compositions, "You're My Peace of Mind." ● Influenced by Philadelphia-based maestro Thom Bell, McCoy also counted Beethoven, Mozart, and Rachmaninoff among his influences and fashioned his own unique approach to making records for the discothèques. Working with production partner Charles Kipps, he helmed two albums for Melba Moore in 1976, which spawned a string of club staples like "This is It," "Free," and "Make Me Believe in You," and recorded with Aretha Franklin and Gladys Knight & the Pips. ● Disco lost one of its most prolific figures when Van McCoy passed suddenly in 1979, leaving more than 700 copyrights to his name at 39 years old. Like the masters he admired, McCoy's influence transcended the era.

DOUBLE EXPOSURE

Double Exposure created a first for the industry: in May 1976, the Philadelphia-based quartet's "Ten Percent" became the first commercially available 12-inch single. Salsoul Records pioneered the release, with DJ Walter Gibbons extending the track to nearly 10 minutes of disco bliss. ● "'Ten Percent' is the perfect choice for this breakthrough move," Vince Aletti declared in *Record World.* "It's a strong record already receiving saturation disco play only weeks after its release; it has great radio crossover potential; and much of its success is due to its length—the sort of nonstop drive that could never be duplicated on a standard 45." ● Building on their success with The Salsoul Orchestra, Salsoul emerged as the top disco label while the title track to Double Exposure's debut for the company created a new paradigm for the industry. "Being headquartered in New York, Salsoul was right there on the scene to get the feel of what was going on," explains MFSB guitarist Bobby Eli, who played on *Ten Percent* (1976). "Salsoul really had their finger on the pulse of disco." ● It was perfect casting for Earl Young—the man who created the quintessential four-on-the-floor disco beat—to play drums on a song that would make history, co-producing it with partners Ronnie Baker and Norman Harris. "Double Exposure signed to us," he says. "They'd been around Philly for a long time. We got a deal and recorded them." ● Lead vocalist Jimmy Williams [left], Charles Whittington, Joe Harris, and Leonard "Butch" Davis had plenty more for the clubs. Following the historic release of "Ten Percent," follow-up singles "My Love is Free" and "Every Man (Has to Carry His Own Weight)" made the Disco Top 20, while *Fourplay* (1978) and *Locker Room* (1979) rounded out the group's time at Salsoul. Even with just "Ten Percent" to their credit, Double Exposure gave more than 100% to the disco era.

DR. BUZZARD'S ORIGINAL SAVANNAH BAND

The Los Angeles Times: "Hottest disco act in the country." *Village Voice*: "A fresh pop hybrid with its own rhythmic integrity." *Rolling Stone*: "Scintillating audacity." ● Dr. Buzzard's Original Savannah Band were welcomed by superlatives from across the music press upon the release of their self-titled debut in 1976. Hailing from the Bronx, the group's unique fusion of styles turned clubs into vivid, technicolor fantasy worlds. "Stony and August wanted to have that image and feel of a big band sound, swing but mixed with Latin, mixed with jazz, and just a whole potpourri of American and World genres," says lead vocalist and co-founder Cory Daye [pictured center, with Coati Mundi, Stony Browder, Jr., Mickey Sevilla, and August Darnell]. ● Produced by Sandy Linzer, "Cherchez La Femme" evoked ballrooms lined with potted palms and mirrored walls. "The lyrics to the songs are all from August Darnell's head," says Daye. "'Cherchez La Femme' was created as a singsong-y type of vocal that really didn't have a lead arrangement to it, and so I just went in and sang. I created that lead vocal arrangement." ● RCA Records nearly abandoned the album, but club promoters Ray and Bob Caviano had a strategy—bring the album to Fire Island. "We went to Fire Island," Daye recalls. "Every house we passed was playing a different cut off the album! They were playing 'Cherchez La Femme' and 'I'll Play the Fool' and 'Sour and Sweet.' By September, we were getting airplay because all of the DJs from Fire Island brought it to The Loft and all the underground clubs. It just shot out... and *then* RCA started promoting." ● The strategy worked. *Record World* declared *Dr. Buzzard's Original Savannah Band* "Most Essential Disco Album of 1976" while the group garnered a GRAMMY nomination for Best New Artist. Gloria Estefan, Queen Latifah, A Tribe Called Quest, and M.I.A. would be among the artists to cover or sample Savannah Band in the coming decades, but nothing could surpass Cory Daye's beguiling vocal performance or the uniqueness of the band's creative vision.

STEVIE WONDER

"Stevie Wonder still is the genius of the 20th century," declares Ray Parker, Jr. In just 10 years, Wonder had grown from Motown's 12-year-old wunderkind to a musical visionary, constantly exploring new sonic frontiers on each album. The 1970s were ripe for experimentation and many of the era's innovations were led by Wonder [pictured with Dance Theater of Harlem]. ● While recording *Music of My Mind* (1972), Wonder began incorporating musical technology that would characterize much of the music popularized in the clubs throughout the decade. "That's one of the first albums that had the synthesized bass on it," says Parker. "Nobody even knew what those sounds were. You couldn't even buy a synthesizer to produce those sounds. They had that big giant TONTO machine that they would plug all the cables into... and that's just to get one sound and one note. It was really groundbreaking territory." ● Wonder's albums had plenty for the DJs, from the tight funk of "Superstition" to the Latin-tinged "Don't You Worry 'Bout a Thing." However, the release of *Songs in the Key of Life* (1976) coincided with disco's ascent as a commercial phenomenon. In his own way, Wonder offered a wealth of danceable pop and R&B that flourished in the discothèques, especially with DJs who had the ingenuity to mix it with other musically innovative cuts. Writing in *Record World*, Vince Aletti noted, "Although its unusual tempo changes make 'Sir Duke' a left-field choice for disco dancing, a number of DJs picked up on it immediately because it blended well with Dr. Buzzard's Original Savannah Band's material." ● Collectively, "Sir Duke," "Another Star," "I Wish," and "Isn't She Lovely" reached the Top 5 of the disco chart, underscoring how Wonder's genius challenged genre categories. The man himself said it in "Sir Duke": "Music is a world within itself."

THELMA HOUSTON

"Disco and dance music has been very good to me," says Thelma Houston. "I've had a great career from it." ● It was Motown Records that catapulted the Mississippi-born singer into the clubs. Though Houston had earned critical acclaim for her debut album *Sunshower* (1969), written and produced by Jimmy Webb, Motown brought Houston's career to new heights upon signing her in 1972. "I *love* Motown," she says. "All of these people that I admired on that label, of *course* I'm going to want to go to Motown!" ● Motown producer Hal Davis knew exactly how to showcase Houston's voice. "I thought Hal was a genius at what he did," she says. "He wanted you to be creative." Houston delivered a tour de force with "Don't Leave Me This Way" on her second Motown album, *Any Way You Like It* (1976). The original version by Harold Melvin & the Blue Notes was barely a year old at the time, yet Hal Davis masterfully amplified the sense of drama that Kenny Gamble and Leon Huff had written into the track. ● "Don't Leave Me This Way" was a revelation for just how well Houston's voice suited the dance milieu. It held the number one spot on the disco chart for six weeks, topped the pop and R&B charts, and won Houston a GRAMMY Award for Best R&B Vocal Performance, Female. She had a lot more for the clubs. Among the highlights, her bracing renditions of "I'm Here Again" and "Love Masterpiece" were featured in the film *Thank God It's Friday* (1978) while the Top 20 hit "Saturday Night, Sunday Morning" opened both *Ready to Roll* (1978) and *Ride to the Rainbow* (1979). Of the artists whose voices defined the era, Houston was truly a commanding force.

THE GIBSON BROTHERS

A Paris-based trio from Martinique inviting listeners to America? That's how the Gibson Brothers introduced themselves on their debut single, "Come to America" (1976). Recorded during the United States' bicentennial, the song sparked a successful relationship between group members [left to right] Patrick Francfort (drums), Chris Francfort (lead vocals), and Alex Francfort (keyboards) with French producer Daniel Vangarde, who named the group and produced their albums on his label, Zagora. The song reached the Top 20 in Italy and Belgium and primed the group's follow-up single "Non-Stop Dance" for the top spot in Belgium and Holland. ● The Gibson Brothers made inroads to North America when T.K. Records released the title track to *Heaven* (1978), which *Record World* described as "another real knockout... the vocals are fine and forceful." However, it was the trio's fourth album *Cuba* (1979) that spawned three club smashes across the globe, including the Latin-inspired title track, "Oooh, What a Life," and "Que Sera Mi Vida (If You Should Go)." The driving, locomotive energy of the track, coupled with Chris Gibson's robust vocals, powered the latter tune to number one in Holland, Denmark, and Belgium, and the Top 5 in Sweden, Switzerland, Germany, and the UK. ● *The Los Angeles Times* sensed the album's club appeal in the US, where both "Cuba" and "Que Sera Mi Vida" rocketed to the Top 10 of the disco chart. "It's no wonder disco DJs are swooning over this record," the newspaper stated. "This is dance music at its most intelligent and irresistible." ● The lilting "Mariana" ushered The Gibson Brothers into the 1980s and back into the Top 20 in the UK and Germany. Wherever dance music led them, The Gibson Brothers left a trail of disco heat on the dance floor.

HEATWAVE

Clubs were already hip to Heatwave when "Boogie Nights" sizzled across the airwaves in the spring of 1977. The group had released their debut *Too Hot to Handle* (1976) on GTO Records in the UK several months earlier. "Loose and sinuous, understated, but right to the point," Vince Aletti observed in *Record World*. "Not the usual disco sound but with more and more records in innovative styles gaining acceptance these days, this one could be a major hit." ● "Major hit" was an understatement. Produced by London-based Barry Blue, "Boogie Nights" shot to number two on both sides of the Atlantic, and established Heatwave as a unique purveyor of streamlined funk. "We were trying to create the heat!" exclaimed Keith Wilder [second from right, back], whose brother Johnnie [*left*] founded the group in Germany after serving in the US Army. "'Boogie Nights' was a jam. We liked the jazz twist to start it off. Nobody expected it. The goal was to create our own brand of pop music or funk music. Me and Johnnie just happened to be from Dayton, Ohio but then all the rest of the band was from Europe. I think it was like a breath of fresh air. We weren't competing with anybody because we were creating our own sound." ● Heatwave's international DNA included English songwriter and keyboardist Rod Temperton [second from left] whose songwriting anchored everything from "Boogie Nights" and "The Groove Line" to the timeless ballad, "Always and Forever." "Rod is a genius writer who accepts no compromise," Barry Blue notes. "He will work a song for months if necessary." Most notably, Temperton quickly emerged as a hit songwriter for Quincy Jones' productions, masterminding The Brothers Johnson's "Stomp!", Michael Jackson's "Rock With You" and later "Thriller", among several other classics. ● Epic Records might have dubbed Heatwave the "English disco sound," but their music defied geography. Heatwave sparked a blaze *everywhere*.

HEATWAVE

BRICK

"Disco jazz" comes from Atlanta, or at least the melding of two distinct musical forms on "Dazz," the chart-topping R&B hit by Brick. Band members Jimmy "Lord" Brown (horns and flute), Ray Ransom (bass), Regi Hargis (guitar), Eddie Irons (drums), and Don Nevins (keyboards) introduced a unique sound to the discothèques that drew on the strengths of what Irons [right] describes as "five individually unorthodox players and writers who approached things completely differently." ● Written by Irons, Ransom, and Hargis, "Dazz" stemmed from the group's 1976 debut LP, *Good High*. "It was definitely a segmented production," notes Irons. "It was an intellectual thought before it was a chorus. Then we made it into a chorus, then made it into a melody, and then made into a singable, memorable hook." ● Performing "Dazz" everywhere from *Soul Train* to an episode of *Saturday Night Live* hosted by Georgia senator Julian Bond, Brick brought Atlanta's fervent music scene to national television. "There was an excellence of Black culture in Atlanta that Brick grew out of," Irons explains. "Atlanta of the '70s for Black music was the same as San Francisco in the '60s. There was a street in Atlanta called Campbellton Road. Bands that were Atlanta bred and born that came out of that era generally had something to do with the clubs that were on that street." ● During an autograph signing at Peaches record store in Atlanta, the band signed a life-size mural of the album cover for their follow-up album *Brick* (1977), which spawned the Top 5 R&B smash, "Dusic." "Our creative energy was on 12 at that point," says Irons. "You come out with your first swing, and hit a home run, it gives you a crazy amount of confidence." Onstage or in the studio, Brick translated that confidence into rock solid grooves.

Love and Happiness
From
Jimmy Brown
Best Wishes

THE RITCHIE FAMILY

Disco got a little more flamboyant when producer Jacques Morali formed The Ritchie Family. Named for Philadelphia-based arranger Richie Rome, the group featured MFSB players who rendered Morali's postcard-inspired fantasies. Featuring Sigma Sound Studio vocalists Barbara Ingram, Carla Benson, and Yvette Benton, the title track to *Brazil* (1975) topped the disco chart for seven weeks and made The Ritchie Family a welcome addition to the clubs. ● In 1976, for the *Arabian Nights* album, Morali and production partner Henri Belolo enlisted [left to right] Cassandra Wooten, Gwen Wesley, and Cheryl Mason-Dorman to record and perform as The Ritchie Family for three albums on T.K.-distributed Marlin Records. Morali created another chart-topping disco smash with "The Best Disco in Town." "It was phenomenal," says Wooten. "Coming from Philadelphia, you hope for a national hit. The *international* success of 'The Best Disco in Town' blew our minds." ● "Henri and Jacques came with a global perspective about where they wanted us to be," adds Mason-Dorman. "They promoted us in all these countries in Europe and South America, Australia, and the Philippines. We weren't family in terms of blood, but we *became* a family, being on the road with each other and doing the things that we did together as The Ritchie Family." ● *Life is Music* (1977), and *African Queens* (1977) kept The Ritchie Family on top, as the latter album crowned the disco chart for three weeks. "We liked the characterizations of Nefertiti, Cleopatra, and Queen of Sheba," says Wooten. "Each of us was very satisfied with the historical person that we were matched with. Everything lined up." Though Morali recast The Ritchie Family for *American Generation* (1978) and subsequently moved the group to Casablanca Records where they appeared in the Village People vehicle *Can't Stop the Music* (1980), the original members created a template that melded an extravagant combination of glamour, soul, and sophistication.

CERRONE

Success came fast for Cerrone. The French drummer and producer had already made an impression in clubs across Europe as a member of the band Kongas, whose creative team also featured disco masters like Don Ray and Alec R. Costandinos. "For my first solo album, I did not want to make any concessions from the music business," Cerrone recalls. "My pleasure and my pride was to put the drums upfront in the mix. No record labels in France wanted to sign me a contract. So, I pressed my vinyl records myself that I sold to wholesalers. One of them was in New York. 'Love in C Minor' was a club hit, so I made an appointment and met Atlantic's Ahmet Ertegun, who offered me a contract immediately." ● Regine's, the famed Park Avenue discothèque, helped break Cerrone in the states. Resident DJ Jonata Garavaglia had made the title track to Cerrone's 1976 solo debut, *Love in C Minor*, a favorite among Manhattan's fabulously attired glitterati. The 17-minute track, which Cerrone penned with Costandinos, put a pulse to the sound of pleasure. ● Amidst his solo success, Cerrone also produced albums for Revelacion (*House of the Rising Sun*) and Don Ray (*The Garden of Love*), and re-teamed with Kongas for *Africanism* (1977). Tracks like "Supernature" and "Give Me Love" powered Cerrone's third album to number one on the disco chart and sealed his renown as one of dance music's most celebrated producers. "I really wanted to stay original," he adds. "As my first two albums had been hits, many productions had a sound close to mine. So, I did 'Supernature,' which corresponded to nothing comparable on the market." Indeed, Cerrone might be the only artist who could make an ecological warning sound sexy on the dance floor.

REGINE'S
510
TAXI
NO
PARKING
TAXI STAND

THE EMOTIONS

In the summer of 1977, no sound was sweeter than The Emotions. Produced by Earth, Wind & Fire founder Maurice White, the platinum-selling "Best of My Love" topped the pop charts for five weeks and brought sisters Wanda, Sheila, and Pamela Hutchinson a GRAMMY Award for "Best R&B Vocal Performance by a Duo or Group." ● White and collaborator Charles Stepney tailored The Emotions' sound to a blend of shimmery pop and soul, starting with *Flowers* (1976), which was their debut on White's ARC label. "I signed them to ARC because of their unique sound and identifiable harmonies," he said. "Working with them gave me a chance to explore a softer, sweeter side of music than was possible with an all-male band. "I Don't Wanna Lose Your Love," written by Wanda Vaughn [middle] and sister Jeanette, was a favorite in the clubs and gave the group a Top 5 disco hit. "It was like a 10-minute song," Wanda recalls. "It was a torch song. I started it off really slow. Maurice said, 'We're going to speed this up! It's too long.' He had an ear for that thing." ● White also knew where to place Wanda's voice in "Best of My Love," which he wrote with EWF guitarist Al McKay for the trio's *Rejoice* (1977) album. "When I started recording it, I started singing it just like Maurice was singing it, in a low key," she recalls. "He said, 'Wanda, you're not singing it in *that* key, you're singing it an octave higher!' I said, 'I don't sing up there all the time. I *end up* there, but I don't usually *start* up there!'" ● "Wanda has that thing that just goes through you," adds McKay. "I knew 'Best of My Love' was a hit, as soon as I heard her open her mouth. The groove and the background vocals... the harmony at the end just about sold the record!" The Emotions' next stop with Earth, Wind & Fire? A trip to "Boogie Wonderland."

SOUL TRAIN

When Cameo arrived in Los Angeles, the New York City-based band were welcomed by Chocolate City, Cecil Holmes' newly formed imprint for Casablanca's R&B division. Cameo's debut single "Find My Way" inaugurated Chocolate City and shot to the Top 5 of the disco chart in 1975. Holmes, along with Casablanca president Neil Bogart, included "Find My Way" on three separate albums, Cameo's full-length debut *Cardiac Arrest* (1977), the soundtrack to *Thank God It's Friday* (1978), and their gold-selling *Secret Omen* (1979). ● "I don't think we ever did another disco song that way," Cameo co-founder and vocalist Tomi Jenkins [top left] laughs about the song. "The whole advent of FM and the clubs becoming a viable source to discover and promote new music made it possible for bands to record six-minute songs and to know that the record label would be able to support it. Our dance songs were a lot more funky—'Rigor Mortis' defined us and really took us away from everything else that was there at the time. 'It's Serious' was more a Cameo-sounding 'disco' song." ● Cameo brought an edgy and irreverent yet compulsively danceable funk-disco hybrid to clubs on songs like "I Just Want to Be," "Macho," and "Shake Your Pants" before dominating the pop charts in the 1980s. With band leader and producer Larry Blackmon driving the grooves, Chocolate City was an ideal home for Cameo. "I can't think of any label that could have been better for us to be at during that time in our career," says Jenkins. "We needed a label that was just like us, that was different, that took chances, that was eclectic, that was out there. ● "It was perfect, man."

Odyssey made the quintessential New York anthem for the disco era: "Native New Yorker." Musically, it evoked Manhattan's twinkling skyline. "When you hear the intro with the sax, it's supposed to be like you're walking through New York streets," says arranger Charlie Calello, who produced the track with Sandy Linzer for Odyssey's 1977 self-titled debut. "It's got the slickness of New York, yet it's got the funk of the street." ● The concept for the song actually originated with another New York group that Linzer had recently produced. "'Native New Yorker' was a title that came to me from working with Dr. Buzzard's Original Savannah Band," he recalls. "It's really written about Cory Daye and what her life was like." Four Seasons writer Denny Randell helped shape the song's vivid storyboard. "There was a certain pulse in the city at that time," he says. "The city had a great bright wonderful vibration to it, musically and socially. The song captures the vibe, and the heart and soul of that city." ● "Native New Yorker" gave sisters Lillian [left] and Louise Lopez their first of several club hits, including the number one UK hit, "Use It Up, Wear It Out." "I loved their personalities," says Linzer, who continued producing the trio after Bill McEachern replaced original member Tony Reynolds [center] on their second album *Hollywood Party Tonight* (1979). "They were very easy to work with. I loved their sound." ● Studio 54 DJ Richie Kaczor loved their sound too, and sequenced "Native New Yorker" for maximum effect during the course of the evening. "One night, my wife and I went there," Linzer recalls. "Midnight comes. Balloons start flying out of the ceiling. Confetti comes down. 'Native New Yorker' comes on and everyone's on the dance floor. ● "I get the chills when I think of it now."

GRACE JONES

On Halloween night, 1976, Grace Jones performed at The Gallery. DJ and club founder Nicky Siano had met Jones through her managers, Sy and Eileen Berlin, and invited her to sing "Sorry" and "That's the Trouble" at the club. "She came," he recalls. "No one knew who she was, but she was fabulous. She's an electrifying performer." It was the singer's first American single... and probably the last night she'd ever be unknown in New York. ● Tom Moulton had produced the single and was tasked with completing Jones' full-length debut, *Portfolio* (1977). "Grace was growing when I started with her," he says. "She had so much drive. She said, 'Whatever it takes.' I'll never forget that." Jones' second single, "I Need a Man" crystallized her reputation as a performer whose daring, theatrical image aligned perfectly with the more outrageous elements of disco. ● "'I Need a Man' was something she'd put out in France," Moulton recalls. "I changed a lot of it. I said, 'Jimmy Stuard is the DJ at 12 West. I'm going to give him an instrumental version of it. If it starts to click, then we'll have you come in one night.' Everybody loved the song. They just didn't know what it was." 12 West hosted the grand unveiling. "Grace starts to sing the intro," Moulton continues. "All you see is the spotlight on her, sitting on this rail. Everybody is just shocked. After the song, everybody's yelling and screaming and Grace goes, 'I don't know about you, honey, but I need a fucking *man*!'" ● "I Need a Man" topped the disco chart for two weeks in May 1977 while her gorgeous rendition of "La Vie En Rose" would become a career-defining song. Jones fêted her breakthrough year in dazzling disco style—a New Year's Eve performance at Studio 54 [pictured]. Working with arrangers like John Davis and Thor Baldursson, Moulton produced two more albums for Jones, *Fame* (1978) and *Muse* (1979), before the singer's critically acclaimed musical reinvention with Sly Dunbar and Robbie Shakespeare in 1980. Combining music, art, videos, and fashion, Jones was more than an artist, she was a fearless icon who transcended all boundaries.

THE BROTHERS JOHNSON

The Brothers Johnson met one of their biggest fans in September 1977. "Michael Jackson introduced the Brothers Johnson at Carnegie Hall," recalls George Johnson [left]. "We didn't know it. We were behind the curtains. He came right onstage. It caught my ear—*This sounds like Michael Jackson*. The curtain opened and it was him. He turned around and smiled at me and Louis." ● At the time, Jackson was in New York working on *The Wiz* (1978) with Quincy Jones, who'd recorded George and Louis Johnson a few years earlier on his album *Mellow Madness* (1975). "I was planning on doing a record by myself," George Johnson recalls. "Quincy said, 'You're going to need a bass player. Your brother can play the shit out of the bass.' Quincy called us The Johnson Brothers. Then we flipped it because the Bee Gees had the Brothers Gibb, so we started The Brothers Johnson." Dubbed "Thunder Thumbs and Lightnin' Licks" for their musical virtuosity, the duo quickly scored two platinum albums, including their aptly named 1976 debut *Look Out for #1*. ● "The real true signature of the Brothers Johnson is the bass and guitar," says Johnson. "I got Louis into the funk when we were young through Sly & the Family Stone. Sly inspired all of my funk, along with James Brown. The funk goes deep." ● Written by The Brothers Johnson with Jones, "Get the Funk Out Ma Face" climbed up the disco chart in 1976 while "I'll Be Good to You" topped the R&B chart. From their gold-selling cover of "Strawberry Letter 23" to their collaboration with Ashford & Simpson on "Ride-O-Rocket," The Brothers Johnson created their own style of funk. However, there was one word that would define the duo's chart-topping apex in the clubs as a new decade beckoned: "Stomp!"

ROSE ROYCE

"Are you serious? You want me to sing a song about a *car wash*?" ● Gwen Dickey, the original lead vocalist of Rose Royce, wasn't sure what to think when producer Norman Whitfield presented the title song he'd written for the film *Car Wash* (1976). "Nobody knows my name and I'm telling *Norman Whitfield* that it's a stupid song," she recalls. "He said, 'You won't say that when you're famous.'" ● Whitfield's prediction came true: "Car Wash" gave Rose Royce a platinum single, topping both the pop and R&B charts in January 1977. It was an auspicious debut for the nine-member band who Whitfield rechristened after signing them to his own eponymous record label. "He wanted a name that represented male and female," Dickey explains. "He said all women like roses and then 'Royce' would be the masculine side of the group. When you see a Rolls Royce driving down the street, you think 'class.' He wanted the group to be about class. I used to be onstage in a Bob Mackie gown with a pair of knee-high boots. Even though you had Rufus & Chaka Khan, it was a different sort of quality compared to ours. We always enjoyed performing together. At that time, it was just magical." ● Rose Royce followed up with more club-ready hits like "Do Your Dance" and "It Makes You Feel Like Dancin'" on *Rose Royce II: In Full Bloom* (1977). "The Rose Royce LP proves that their phenomenal out-of-the-blue success with the *Car Wash* soundtrack was no fluke," *Record World* wrote. "They've inspired producer Norman Whitfield's best album work since his peak years with The Temptations." From the car wash to the disco, Rose Royce had a groove for any occasion.

D.C. LaRUE

Flamingo, Infinity, and 12 West were among the discothèques that ruled gay nightlife during the mid-1970s... and there was D.C. LaRue standing in front of each of them on the back cover to his debut album, *Ca-the-drals* (1976). Written and co-produced by LaRue, the title track peaked at #2 on *Billboard*'s Disco Singles Chart, a surprise hit for record impresario Morris Levy, who distributed the singer's label, Pyramid Records. ● "On Monday, I was unknown. Two weeks later I had the number one dance record in the city," LaRue recalls. "I wasn't getting any radio play, and I was selling hundreds of thousands of records. I remember Morris scratching his head saying, 'I've never seen anything like this in my life.'" ● LaRue knew the disco scene as a participant, observer, and recording artist, channeling that combination into a cool, sometimes ironic, perspective that resonated with dancers and DJs alike. Months after scoring his first disco hit, he returned to the Top 5 with selections from his second album *The Tea Dance* (1976), making him one of dance music's most intriguing new artists. ● "I had a New York City mystique that nobody could figure out," says LaRue, who relocated to LA after signing with Casablanca Records. The label teamed him with Bob Esty, who produced a pair of tracks for LaRue in *Thank God It's Friday* (1978), plus *Confessions* (1978) and *Forces of the Night* (1979). "It was just an ideal situation," says LaRue, whose "Let Them Dance" launched his first hit for the label. "Nobody told me what to do. I went into record *Forces of the Night* and it was like 'Spend whatever you want to spend!'" For an artist who featured everyone from Lou Christie to Rita Moreno on his albums, Casablanca was a musical promised land.

ROY AYERS

"I try to be everywhere and play everything," Roy Ayers told *Billboard* in December 1976. "Right now, I'm aiming at the pop market and anything that encompasses R&B and jazz." At the suggestion of his manager, Ayers even dubbed his group Roy Ayers Ubiquity to reflect his expansive approach to recording. ● Ayers was among jazz musicians like George Benson, Harvey Mason, and Herbie Hancock who'd begun fusing more pronounced, R&B-oriented rhythms with their music. Over a 12-month period, the vibraphonist released a trio of albums—*Everybody Loves the Sunshine* (1976), *Vibrations* (1976), and *Lifeline* (1977)—that captured him at his height as the leader of Roy Ayers Ubiquity and solidified his appeal in the discothèques. The thunderous grooves of "Come Out and Play" teased listeners with a coy invitation, "Come out of the closet and play," which suggested a whole other meaning in the gay clubs. ● While the sublimely mellow "Everybody Loves the Sunshine" would define Ayers' career—"It's like my national anthem," he'd later say—"Running Away" became Ayers' most indelible recording for the clubs. Its rubbery rhythm and infectious hook powered the song to #14 on the disco chart. Even as Ayers continued to record songs with lyrics that explicitly reflected dancing, "Get On Up, Get On Down" and "Heat of the Beat," and revisited earlier tracks like "Sweet Tears" and "When is Real, Real?" with a disco pulse, "Running Away" remained his gold standard for the clubs. ● "My music has always been danceable," Ayers said years later, crediting James Brown as a primary influence. "People want to be free and express themselves. They want to groove, man." And the sound of Ayers' groove could be summed up in six syllables: "do-be-do / run run run."

ALEC R. COSTANDINOS

Saint Tropez, summer 1977. Composer and producer Alec R. Costandinos is relaxing after a prolific period of writing and recording. "Accidental Lover" and "I Found Love (Now That I Found You)" from the self-titled debut of his studio group *Love & Kisses* (1977) top the disco chart for three weeks in July 1977. His next project, *Sphinx* (1977), brings the Biblical figures of "Judas Iscariot" and "Simon Peter" to the discothèques that same month. He's also about to record *Sumeria: Golden Tears* (1977), a disco saga about a "cosmic traveler" who's sent to earth to experience love and mortality. ● The inspiration for Costandinos' next album, *Romeo & Juliet* (1978), bloomed in the South of France, and would become the most vaunted of his disco masterpieces. "My routine became more intense with every passing day," he recalls about the process of composing the piece. "At times, I could see the characters, and I would be transported into a scene where I became an imaginary protagonist. Or I would see Romeo and Juliet as a futuristic ballet, and I was the only spectator sitting in the center row of a very large theatre." ● Costandinos presented *Romeo & Juliet* to Casablanca Records, who credited the album as "Alec R. Costandinos & the Syncophonic Orchestra." *Record World* deemed it the producer's "most accomplished and fully satisfying work... a moving, important album" while dancers savored how Costandinos and arranger Don Ray orchestrated the star-crossed story in five acts. *Romeo & Juliet* topped the disco chart in March 1978, where Costandinos would soon return as the composer and producer of Love & Kisses' theme to *Thank God It's Friday* (1978). ● "The idea is to keep the music as interesting as possible," the producer later shared at *Billboard*'s Disco Forum in March 1979. In that endeavor, Alec R. Costandinos always excelled. He remains disco's consummate auteur.

PETER BROWN

It had to happen—the first 12-inch single to be certified gold. And it happened to Peter Brown. His first release for T.K. Records, "Do You Wanna Get Funky With Me?" reached the million-selling mark in September 1977. ● Co-produced by Brown with T-Connection producer Cory Wade, the song immediately caught fire in the clubs upon its release during the spring of 1977. "The most outrageous, adventuresome, and off-the-wall production of the year," Vince Aletti wrote in *Record World*. "Brown and Wade have concocted an eight-minute masterpiece of funk disco with a series of vocal and instrumental segments, each more intense and explosive than the one before. The record unfolds rather unexpectedly, like a pot of water gradually heating up and boiling over." ● Brown had arranged and played most of the instruments on the smoldering track and summoned a gritty vocal that belied his more unassuming personality. "He's a great dude. Unbelievably talented," says T-Connection member Theo Coakley. "He's such a quiet guy, and he has a quiet voice, but when he sings 'Do you wanna get funky with me?' it's like Clark Kent and Superman!" ● *Record World* named Brown #1 New Male Vocalist, in the category of R&B Singles for 1977 before he released his full-length debut *A Fantasy Love Affair* later that year. A crew from *60 Minutes* documented Brown in the studio with vocalist Betty Wright at an overdubbing session for his follow-up single, "Dance With Me." The song would reach the Top 10 and earn him a GRAMMY nomination for "Best R&B Vocal Performance, Male" plus a *Billboard* award for "Top New Male Albums Artist" (1978). Brown capped the 1970s with another Top 5 dance hit, "Crank It Up (Funk Town)," cementing him as one of the era's most prodigious talents.

TAVARES

Five brothers, one name, timeless music. Tiny, Pooch, Butch, Chubby, and Ralph Tavares brought a sweet and smooth vocal blend to the dance floor. During the early-'70s, the New England-based vocal quintet had established themselves as soulful balladeers with songs like "Check It Out," "Remember What I Told You to Forget," and a number one R&B cover of Hall & Oates' "She's Gone." "It Only Takes a Minute," a track from their third Capitol album *In the City* (1975), brought Tavares a second number one hit and also broadened their presence in the clubs. ● *Sky-High!* (1976) was the perfect title for their next album. Produced by Freddie Perren, it spawned two #1 disco classics, "Don't Take Away the Music" and the gold-selling "Heaven Must Be Missing An Angel." It also preceded a major moment in their career. ● "The Bee Gees came out to see us performing at Madison Square Garden," Ralph Tavares recalled years later in an interview with *UK Music Reviews*. "We saw these gentlemen coming down the tunnel after the show was over and we were all trying to work out just who they were. However, as they got closer we realized that it was The Bee Gees. They were ranting, raving, applauding, and laughing about what they had just seen during the show. They said to us at the time, 'We are doing a movie, it's called *Saturday Night Fever* and we would like to have you guys involved with the movie. We are currently writing a song especially for you.' At first, we all thought that they were just making conversation and just being polite and then they went off. Some months later, our manager called us and told us that The Bee Gees wanted us to sing 'More Than A Woman' in the movie." Sky-high, indeed.

BEE GEES

Barry Gibb has a philosophy about writing songs. "Creative visualization," he says. "You have to imagine something finished before you start doing it. You've got to have a picture in your head, and in your heart, of what it's going to be like when it's done before you embark on *how* it's done." ● Could Barry Gibb and brothers Robin and Maurice have envisioned how "Stayin' Alive," "Night Fever," and "How Deep is Your Love" would start the Bee Gees' string of six consecutive number one singles, or turn the *Saturday Night Fever* (1977) soundtrack into a best-selling behemoth? ● A danceable strand of pop had already reinvigorated the Bee Gees' sound on *Main Course* (1975). Working with producer Arif Mardin, "Jive Talkin'" seemed a universe away from late-'60s hits like "To Love Somebody," though the trio's love for R&B remained a consistent influence in their songwriting. "We were always exploring how else we could experiment," says Gibb. Barry Gibb's falsetto on "Nights on Broadway" introduced a new texture to the Bee Gees' records and would anchor their biggest hits, including the explosive "You Should Be Dancing" on *Children of the World* (1976). ● Almost unwittingly, the Bee Gees perfected a pop-disco hybrid on *Saturday Night Fever*, plus the chart-topping songs they wrote and produced for younger brother Andy Gibb. "They weren't just tapping into the zeitgeist as they had been with 'You Should Be Dancing' two years earlier," *The Guardian* noted. "Now the zeitgeist emanated from Criteria Studios in Miami, and from the Gibb brothers themselves." ● *Saturday Night Fever* won a GRAMMY Award for "Album of the Year" and catapulted the Bee Gees into a stratosphere of rarefied, 25x platinum success. And with the release of their *Spirits Having Flown* (1979) album, the fever kept rising...

YVONNE ELLIMAN

Legendary lyricist Sir Tim Rice knew Yvonne Elliman long before "Fever" mania. She originated "Mary Magdalene" in the rock opera *Jesus Christ Superstar* (1970), which Rice penned with Sir Andrew Lloyd Webber. "Yvonne had a beautiful, pure voice," he says. "She didn't quite sound like anybody else." She's also that rare vocalist who could sing everything from The Who to the Bee Gees with equal authority. ● In fact, the Bee Gees were label mates with Elliman on RSO Records, where they penned the title track to her fourth solo album, *Love Me* (1976) produced by Freddie Perren. However, it was Elliman's version of the trio's "If I Can't Have You" that brought an emotional resonance to *Saturday Night Fever* (1977). Perren turned the song into three minutes of torch-inflected disco. "I love 'If I Can't Have You,'" Tom Moulton exclaims. "I like the emotion that Yvonne put into it. There was nothing else like it on *Saturday Night Fever*. It's got a little bit of that delay, hesitation in the beat." ● "If I Can't Have You" followed the Bee Gees' "Night Fever" to the top of the Hot 100 in May 1978, the fourth chart-topping single from the soundtrack. "I was lying in bed," Elliman recalls. "I remember getting a call from RSO. 'Guess what, Yvonne? You're number one with a bullet!' I remember getting in the car and hearing it on the radio. It was a tremendous high." ● The success of "If I Can't Have You" prompted an image makeover for the singer—"RSO took away my jeans and put me in red satin pants and chain mail tops!" Elliman duly complied and enjoyed another club hit in 1979 with "Love Pains," a deceptively flashy tale of romantic woe. Only Yvonne Elliman could turn heartache into a dance floor classic.

COMMODORES

"Six guys with six different types of music they loved." That's how Commodores co-founder William "WAK" King [third from left] described band mates Thomas McClary [left], Lionel Richie [second from left], Ronald LePread [right], Walter "Clyde" Orange, and Milan Williams in a *Cryptic Rock* magazine interview. The influence of blues, jazz, funk, pop ballads, hard rock, and big band coalesced into a unified sound that gave the Commodores four consecutive platinum number one albums on the R&B chart from 1976–1979. "We had a huge amount of ingredients to throw into one pot. We were just all over the place. It was great and sometimes we surprised ourselves." ● Within a few years of forming the group at Tuskegee University in Alabama and touring with the Jackson 5, the Commodores' music flourished in the discos. The instrumental title track to their Motown debut *Machine Gun* (1974), plus "Slippery When Wet," which topped the R&B chart in 1975, and "Fancy Dancer," laid the foundation for the group's gold-selling classic "Brick House" in 1977. "We needed one more song to go on the album, so everybody started throwing licks and things into the pot," King recalled about the latter song. "That song almost didn't make it on the album. It wasn't until Walter Orange took it into the studio to put a vocal over the track that we already cut that gave the song incredible life." ● "Brick House" was also among the Commodores songs featured in the Casablanca-Motown film *Thank God It's Friday* (1978). Onscreen, the group performed another #1 R&B hit, "Too Hot Ta Trot," during the dance contest sequence filmed at Osko's in Los Angeles for the movie's fictional Zoo Disco. Even as the Commodores topped the pop charts with Lionel Richie's timeless ballads, they still appealed to the clubs, especially on the title track to *Midnight Magic* (1979) where they invited listeners "down to the disco." From funk to pop, The Commodores were always in command of the groove.

DONNA SUMMER

Donna Summer could sing it *all*. The disco era was an ideal showcase for her musical versatility and her singular approach to singing. Every six months between 1975 and 1979, Summer topped the disco chart with a classic produced by Giorgio Moroder and Pete Bellotte, while also unveiling a new artistic persona, from the provocative "First Lady of Love" on *Love to Love You Baby* (1975) to the glamorous "Disco Cinderella" of *Once Upon a Time* (1977), to the sassy rock 'n' roll belter on *Bad Girls* (1979). ● "I would consider myself much more of an actress, in some ways, than a singer because I think that each song is a little mini movie," she said. "Giorgio was very clever in that he said, 'Donna, you're going to be marketed just as a *singer*. We're going to promote you in a way that people will play your records on all kinds of radio stations.' He worked very hard at getting me to cross over. I just had to show up, but that was really more of a marketing thing from the record company." ● Casablanca Records launched Summer to superstardom in 1975, sparking one of the most prolific careers in popular music. "I started with 'Love to Love You Baby'—that was sort of a fluke—but I came out of musical theater and I was used to belting," she explained. "They realized that I was actually much more savvy in music than they had thought." Summer's stunning vocal performances on the Oscar-winning "Last Dance" and "MacArthur Park" revealed a power and range that surpassed the clubs while the platinum success of "Hot Stuff" and "Bad Girls" burnished her renown as one of the most successful solo artists of all time. ● The key to Summer's success? "I don't limit myself."

1978–1979

"Disco music is very fresh. It's alive," declares Tina Turner. "I respect the music very much." It's 1979 and Turner's a guest on *Musical Express* in Spain. Alec R. Costandinos has just produced her album *Love Explosion* (1979). She's also added a showstopping rendition of "Disco Inferno" to her live show. A few artists, in particular, have caught the singer's attention. "Grace Jones, Amanda Lear, Donna Summer... I think this is very good for this new group of people with this type of music."

Disco was also very good for rock. In 1978, The Rolling Stones and Rod Stewart both recorded songs that not only topped the pop chart but would stand among the biggest hits of their careers. Though rock textures weren't necessarily new in dance music, whether the gritty vocals of Barrabás or T-Connection's blistering "On Fire," the success of established rock artists in the disco realm solidified dance music's appeal across multiple genres of music.

Of course, *Saturday Night Fever* made disco ubiquitous. The film's soundtrack began a staggering 24-week reign at number one in January 1978, selling more than a half a million units *per day*. From "Stayin' Alive" to "More Than a Woman," the songs that Barry, Robin, and Maurice Gibb wrote and recorded were key to the album's unprecedented sales. "Records today help sell movies and vice versa," *The New York Times* reported at the time. "Media interlock ever more tightly, and the beneficiary of the moment is the Bee Gees.

"What Barry and his brothers have done is blend two styles that might have been considered antithetical—disco urgency and lush, middle-of-the-road romanticism. The tunes are lush but tight, and the production is rich and multi-textured yet never murky. And the actual sound of Barry and the others' voices has a husky, plaintive vibrato that is both telling and instantly identifiable."

In the wake of *Saturday Night Fever,* disco ruled the Top 5 on a weekly basis. "Disco is now radio music with a beat," producer and arranger John Davis told *Billboard.* CHIC, Blondie, A Taste of Honey, Michael Jackson, Amii Stewart, Gloria Gaynor, and Anita Ward were among the acts who topped the Hot 100 with disco in 1979, while Donna Summer made history as the first female solo artist to score three number one pop singles in less than a year's time with "MacArthur Park," "Hot Stuff," and "Bad Girls."

Summer's recording of "Last Dance," written by Paul Jabara for the film *Thank God It's Friday* (1978), had already showcased the sheer power and range of her voice, a revelation for those only familiar with "Love to Love You Baby" and "I Feel Love." "The one thing in my career that I can't forget was the night 'Last Dance' was recorded," she shared years later. "We'd been in the studio all night long. I was waiting for them to give me a mix. I just could not go home. The sun was coming up. They used to have these spots on Mulholland Drive that you could pull in and overlook the city. I pull in and I play the music as loud as I could. I get out of the car and I'm dancing around. I drove up some place else and listened to it. I just didn't know what to do with myself. I was like, *This is it!*" "Last Dance" not only earned Summer her first GRAMMY Award, it also won the Oscar for "Best Original Song" and became a pop standard.

CHIC joined Donna Summer and the Bee Gees at number one. Led by writers and producers Nile Rodgers and Bernard Edwards, CHIC parlayed their debut's chart-topping club success with "Everybody Dance" and "Dance, Dance, Dance (Yowsah, Yowsah, Yowsah)" into platinum sales for their second album, *C'est CHIC* (1978). "Le Freak" crowned the Hot 100 for six weeks, becoming the biggest single in the history of Atlantic Records, followed only months later by "Good Times" off *Risqué* (1979).

The New York-based group's fans also included fellow artists. "We always liked CHIC," says Debbie Harry. "Their playing was so great. It was a unique composition and blend of different things. They were influenced by all kinds of music. It did have a very jazzy quality to it." Nona Hendryx adds, "There were a zillion disco and dance records, but CHIC stood out for Nile's guitar and Bernard's solid bass, and songs whose verse, chorus, and bridge were all 'hooks.' Not a traditional mix."

Critics unanimously praised CHIC, especially their production of *We Are Family* (1979) for Sister Sledge. "Bernard Edwards and Nile Rodgers have distilled disco down to its seductive essentials," wrote *The New York Times*. "There's not a single synthesizer here. The result is a spare, spacious elegance... Kathy Sledge is among the most versatile singers ever to assay disco. The extended conclusion of the title track is a tour de force of breathy invocations, hoarse grunts and soprano whoops, a celebration of family that extends and embraces the audience with the fervor of gospel music. Like the best disco music, it not only fulfills its dancing function but transcends it as well, so that it is not merely good disco, but good music."

Paradise Garage was among the clubs that kept CHIC in heavy rotation. Having opened in New York's Hudson Square neighborhood in January 1978, it became a prime gathering place for those seeking a dynamic experience on the dance floor without the paparazzi-focused factions of other clubs. Within a year, *New York Magazine* named resident DJ Larry Levan among "The New Disco Elite" for thrilling crowds with marathon sets while translating his talent to mixing songs like Instant Funk's "I Got My Mind Made Up (You Can Get It Girl)," which topped the R&B and disco charts.

"Larry Levan was the first superstar DJ," *The Guardian* later declared. "His uncanny ability to mix and tweak records for maximum emotional impact would regularly send his devoted congregation into raptures." As New York DJ François K told *VICE*, "Larry had a very charismatic approach to music. When he played a song, you felt like he was playing it for you. That's a remarkable feeling. While Larry owed a huge debt to people like David Mancuso and Nicky Siano, he became this foundational figure."

Meanwhile, DJs tailored their mixes for the roller disco scene as skaters from Venice Beach to Brooklyn's Empire Rollerdrome glided freely on four wheels. DJ Danny Krivit, who spun at the Roxy in New York, explained to *Wax Poetics*: "At the skate clubs, they had a very specific idea of what perfect skating music was. It was a certain tempo and didn't get too fast or slow...which was why [CHIC's] 'Good Times' was such a big song. There was this thing where it wasn't just beat-clap kind of rhythm but an extra-pronounced beat or snare so when you were skating it propelled you and gave you an extra footing."

With disco at its commercial peak, a range of new record companies, including Prelude, Solar, SAM, Total Experience, West End, and Ray Caviano's RFC imprint for Warner Bros., kept dance music thriving in the clubs while artists bridged the 1980s with undeniable dance grooves. Michael Jackson, Blondie, Queen, Lipps, Inc., Diana Ross, and Kool & the Gang all topped the Hot 100 in 1980, showing how the influence of disco would continue well into the new decade. Even as popular tastes evolved, and dance music reshaped itself, nothing could keep the disco ball from spinning.

VILLAGE PEOPLE

"Darling, qu'est-ce que c'est 'Y.M.C.A.'?" French producer Jacques Morali's question turned into a multi-platinum answer. ● "One of the guys said, 'It's Young Men's Christian Association,'" recalls Village People co-founder Felipe Rose, the group's original Native American. Village People had already merged their club appeal with Top 40 radio, but their third album, *Cruisin'* (1978), would catapult them to an entirely new stratosphere of success and visibility. "We needed one more song to finish the album," Rose continues. "Neil Bogart heard 'Y.M.C.A' and he threw it to the front of the line." ● Casablanca Records welcomed Village People to the Casbah. Produced by Morali and Henri Belolo, their 1977 debut celebrated gay haunts like Fire Island, San Francisco, and Hollywood. It topped the disco chart for seven weeks in the fall of 1977 while becoming a rallying antidote to Anita Bryant's "Save Our Children" campaign that demonized gay men. "The album became the soundtrack to the PRIDE parade that year, which was the Christopher Street Liberation Day Parade," says Rose. ● Village People's second album *Macho Man* (1978) crystallized the group's classic line-up featuring Rose, original lead vocalist Victor Willis (cop), Alex Briley (G.I.), David Hodo (construction worker), Randy Jones (cowboy), and Glenn Hughes (biker). "What Casablanca did with their amazing marketing machine and their PR people, Marc Paul Simon and Steven Keator, they then sold Village People as this butch, real masculine group to mainstream America for a general audience," says Rose. ● By the time Village People triumphed at the American Music Awards and appeared on the cover of *Rolling Stone* in 1979, their walls glimmered with gold and platinum records. They conquered the mainstream by boldly subverting masculine archetypes with a wink. Indeed, these six macho men had something for everyone.

T-CONNECTION

T-Connection made history because of disco. When the band's "Do What You Wanna Do" topped the disco chart for seven weeks in spring 1977, they became the first Bahamian band to score a number one on *any* chart in the US. "I used to buy *Billboard* magazine," says band founder, songwriter and keyboardist Theo Coakley, who sang lead on the track. "It was number one at *every single club*. It was an exciting time." ● The song's success delivered on Coakley's vision. "I wanted to put together a group that could get onto the international scene," he says. "I wanted people to dance. I like grooves, man. The music was going to be an R&B base, with island and pop music. I was going to add anything I felt on top." ● Signed to T.K. Records, Coakley [far right] and bandmates Kirk Coakley [second from left], Berkley Van Byrd (drums), Monty Brown (guitar) [third from left], Tony Flowers (percussion), and David Mackey [far left] combined several styles on their second album *On Fire* (1977), including the junkanoo-tinged "Let Yourself Go" and the scorching title track, which bridged rock and classical. "When I was in those big disco clubs, and the people were going crazy, it was like they were on fire," he says. "I wanted to create this *big* track. I had synthesizer breaks, piano breaks, drum breaks, conga breaks... We used the New York Philharmonic string section. It was just fantastic." ● In 1978, Coakley shifted the spotlight to Berkley Van Byrd on "At Midnight", another of the band's Top 5 disco hits. "I wrote it for him because I knew that he's the only guy in the group that can sing at that range," he recalls. "He just *killed* it in the studio!" True to the song's intention, T-Connection came alive at midnight... and *any* time of night.

Marshall
Marshall

SYLVESTER

London, 1978. The Embassy Club on Old Bond Street in the city's West End is the setting for Sylvester's "You Make Me Feel (Mighty Real)" video [pictured]. Lights flash, mirror balls spin, and the singer slowly saunters down the club's staircase, blinking lights illuminating his boots. Attired in black leather, he then morphs into a stylish dandy with white suit and pants before revealing a sparkling, multi-colored robe and turban. He is shapeshifting personified. ● Co-written by Sylvester, with synth master Patrick Cowley creating a cyclone of pulsating synths, "You Make Me Feel (Mighty Real)" combined soul, gospel, passion, and regal disco flair. *Village Voice* critic Robert Christgau described it as "one of those surges of sustained, stylized energy that is disco's great gift to pop music." Coupled with "Dance (Disco Heat)," which featured Two Tons O' Fun vocalists Martha Wash and Izora Rhodes, "You Make Me Feel" topped the disco chart for six weeks in 1978 and powered Sylvester's *Step II* (1978) to gold certification. ● The San Francisco-based artist had long been part of the city's art and rock vanguard, as both a member of The Cockettes and through his own Sylvester & the Hot Band. However, his six solo albums for Fantasy Records coronated his reign as disco royalty, from his rousing cover of Ashford & Simpson's "Over and Over" on his solo debut to his riveting concert album *Living Proof* (1979). "I loved Sylvester's version," says Valerie Simpson. "He took it and did it his way." ● Fellow artists were among Sylvester's most ardent fans. "I used to go see Sylvester when it was Sylvester and Two Tons O' Fun," recalls Thelma Houston. "I loved his shows. He could really, really sing and he had that gospel thing down pat." Indeed, it doesn't get more "mighty real" than Sylvester.

EXIT

AMANDA LEAR

David Bowie and Rolling Stones member Brian Jones romanced her. Salvador Dalí and Paco Rabanne were besotted with her. Roxy Music immortalized her on the cover to *For Your Pleasure* (1973). A prolific painter and former *VOGUE* model, Amanda Lear was the disco era's glamorous chanteuse. Flipping her long tresses like Tina Turner, Lear purred lyrics with the allure of an exotic feline. ● "My career as a singer was more about acting than anything else," Lear said years later, speaking to *The GROUND* magazine. "I would have never believed it if someone told me that one day I'd sell millions of records. When I started on Italian TV, I couldn't even speak Italian properly. Can you imagine [that] with my voice? It was ridiculous, and yet, it worked out." ● *I Am a Photograph* (1977), the singer's debut album for Ariola Records, marked the first of five albums Lear recorded with German producer Anthony Monn. The album featured some of her biggest hits, including the number one Italian hit "Tomorrow" and "Queen of Chinatown," which reached the Top 5 in Germany, Italy, and Switzerland, plus "Blood and Honey." "The hook here is Lear's deep throated, mysterious vocals shrouded in a hypnotic throbbing backbeat," *Billboard* noted about the latter song. *Record World* described it, simply, as "perfectly decadent." ● "Perfectly decadent" could have also captioned the cover of *Sweet Revenge* (1978), with Lear smiling mischievously while gripping a whip. Lear wrote the lyrics for the entire album, including "Follow Me," an ethereal masterpiece that became a multi-million selling single across Europe and one of Lear's signature recordings. Decades later, the singer herself would cite "The Sphinx" from *Never Trust a Pretty Face* (1979), as the song that best represents who she is: a constantly evolving artist inclined to remain a mystery.

BONEY M.

Boney M. formed in Munich but was destined to conquer the world. German producer Frank Farian brought together an international group of vocalists and dancers, including Liz Mitchell (Jamaica), Marcia Barrett (Jamaica), Maizie Williams (Montserrat), and Bobby Farrell (Aruba), who turned Boney M. into one of the best-selling global acts of the 1970s. ● Farian hatched the group's name from the title character in the Australian television show, *Boney*. "Every discothèque in town wanted to have Boney M.," recalled Mitchell, speaking about the group's success with their debut, *Take the Heat Off Me* (1976). Within months of its release, the album's breakout single "Daddy Cool" propelled Boney M. to number one in Germany, plus the Top 10 in Australia and the UK. In the states, *Record World* described the track as "a freaky, solidly disco production with some slightly jarring commercial touches." Often photographed in provocative attire, Boney M. joined Silver Convention and Donna Summer as alluring icons of the Munich-styled Eurodisco sound typified by melodic string lines and crisp, teutonic beats. ● Before long, Boney M. expanded their audience from the discothèques with a continental, radio-friendly pop sound. Barrett (*left*) and Mitchell (*right*) recorded all of the group's lead vocals, creating a signature vocal blend that anchored other chart-topping hits across Europe like "Sunny," "Ma Baker," "Belfast," "Rasputin," and "Gotta Go Home." Their third album *Nightflight to Venus* (1978) included a lilting version of "Rivers of Babylon," which still stands among the Top 10 Best-Selling UK Singles of All Time. "Every time Boney M. released something it was like, 'Boney M. has done it again!" Williams later recalled. "'*Top of the Pops*—here they come!' ● "When you're on *Top of the Pops*, you know you have arrived."

MICHAEL ZAGER BAND

A photography studio overlooks the Hudson River. Makeup artists and hair stylists prepare models Lisa Taylor and Darlanne Fluegel for a photo shoot. Suddenly, Studio 54 regular Sterling St. Jacques twirls around to the sound of "Let's All Chant" by Michael Zager Band. His joy is infectious. ● This sequence from *Eyes of Laura Mars* (1978) captures how "Let's All Chant" set the soundtrack for a fusion of glamour, music, dance, and fashion, with just a sprinkling of decadence. At the time, Studio 54's resident DJ Richie Kaczor [right] regularly drove dancers into swirls of ecstasy with the track's command to "move your body." ● Michael Zager [second from left] had already broken the club market two years earlier with vocalist Peabo Bryson on the Top 5 disco hit "Do It With Feeling," plus productions for Cissy Houston, Andrea True Connection, and Love Child's Afro Cuban Blues Band, but it was "Let's All Chant" that powered him to the top of the disco chart. He collaborated with session vocalist Alvin Fields, who sang the track's hook with Dolette McDonald and Billy Baker. "My partner, Jerry Love [left], frequented the clubs almost every night and he would tell me what dancers were reacting to," Zager recalls. "He heard dancers in the clubs going 'oo-ah oo-ah.' He said to write a dance song incorporating that mantra. I told him that it was a ridiculous idea. Thank goodness I listened to him." ● To promote the record, Zager visited discothèques with Jerry Love and disco promo mastermind Doug Riddick [second from right]. In fact, midtown club New York, New York would furnish the cover for Zager's follow-up *Life's A Party* (1978). The album was also notable for introducing a vocalist whose voice would soar through clubs in the decade to come—Whitney Houston.

The Michael Zager Band
LET'S ALL CHANT
KAZOR

A TASTE OF HONEY

A Taste Of Honey had several reasons to boogie in 1978. They had a platinum debut album on Capitol Records while their million-selling single "Boogie Oogie Oogie" topped the pop, R&B, and disco charts on its way to platinum certification. ● The victory was years in the making. Producers Larry Mizell and Fonce Mizell had introduced band members [left to right] Perry Kibble (keyboards), Janice-Marie Johnson (bass), Hazel Payne (guitar), and Donald Ray Johnson (drums) to Larkin Arnold, who founded and presided over Capitol's Black Music Division. "He took a chance on us when a lot of people passed on us," says Janice-Marie. "Getting signed had to be one of the most exciting experiences ever. We had been trying to get that for six years." ● It was Larkin Arnold who also shared the news of the group's conquest on the charts. "We were touring with the Commodores," Janice-Marie recalls. "Larkin called me and he was so excited. He said, 'You are number one in *Billboard.*' I said, 'Great! We're number one in *Billboard*... Larkin, what's *Billboard*?' I hadn't had time to worry about the charts or the radio. I was just trying to make sure I knew where our equipment was!" ● The LA-based quartet's sound was steeped in pop and soul with disco and jazz inflections, a quality that shone radiantly at the Shrine Auditorium on the evening of the 21st GRAMMY Awards where they performed their chart-topping hit, penned by Janice-Marie and Perry Kibble. Applause erupted from the audience when John Denver and Eubie Blake presented A Taste Of Honey with the GRAMMY for "Best New Artist." "I was so happy and totally overwhelmed," says Janice-Marie. "You're talking about a complete surprise." Victory never tasted so sweet.

GIORGIO MORODER

Donna Summer was the perfect muse for Giorgio Moroder. "We had great regard for each other's talent," she said. "Giorgio's strength was his music. That was his absolute strength and his vision. He is a brilliant composer." Of course, Moroder's brilliance shaped countless hits that he co-produced with Pete Bellotte during Summer's ascent at Casablanca Records. ● Moroder's own albums teemed with experimentation. *Knights in White Satin* (1976) spawned the Top 5 disco hit "I Wanna Funk With You Tonite" while *From Here to Eternity* (1977) joined Summer's "I Feel Love" as a sonically groundbreaking piece of work. "Giorgio was always evolving," says Bellotte, who also produced albums by Roberta Kelly and Munich Machine with Moroder. "If you ever went up to his house, he was always tinkering on the piano. Because he was always playing and creating, it would be impossible for him not to strike off on different tangents." Arranger and producer Harold Faltermeyer concurs. "It was always his thing to try 10 different effect boxes and put them together," he says. "The needles would bend on the machines. It was a playground he loved to explore." ● Moroder's score for the film *Midnight Express* (1978) introduced him to the biggest playground of all — Hollywood. It also won the Academy Award for "Best Original Score." "Winning the Oscar for *Midnight Express* was one of my most incredible days in my life," he says. "Not only had I never dreamed of winning one but then it came almost too fast!" His film scores for *Foxes* (1980) and *American Gigolo* (1980) quickly followed his own albums, *Battlestar Galactica* (1978) and *E=MC2* (1979), plus a remarkably prolific period where he produced Sparks, Janis Ian, Japan, The Sylvers, The Three Degrees, and Suzi Lane, who topped the disco chart with "Harmony." And with *Flashdance* (1983) on the horizon, Moroder had yet another Oscar waiting for him.

CONTROLLERS
OSCILLATOR BANK
MIXER

HERBIE HANCOCK

Herbie Hancock had a message for fans and critics who questioned his exploration of disco. "I know some of them won't be able to believe I'm playing this kind of music," he told *Billboard*. "They should just sit back and take it for what it is." Anyone who listened heard a master at play in the land of mirror balls. ● Hancock had successfully bridged jazz and funk earlier in the decade on tracks like "Chameleon," "Doin' It," and his re-recording of "Watermelon Man" before cutting a series of albums in the late-'70s that were clearly influenced by the four-on-the-floor stylings of disco. Using the Sennheiser Vocoder VSM201—a synthesizer specifically used with the voice—*Sunlight* (1978) marked Hancock's first vocal album. It also spawned his first Top 20 hit in the UK, "I Thought It Was You," a glistening track designed for spinning and gliding across the dance floor. ● *Feets Don't Fail Me Now* (1979) only amplified the disco quotient, especially on "You Bet Your Love," which featured the legendary vocal group The Waters and gave the musician another major UK hit. "I look at us as being a horn section in the band or the orchestra," says Luther Waters. "The horns have to be tight in a band. That crispness is who we are when we sing. We could sing the notes Herbie played like a horn section." ● The GRAMMY-nominated "Ready Or Not" further illustrated Hancock's renown for musical innovation. "When I think of Herbie Hancock, I think of his genius," says Oren Waters, who sang lead on "Go For It" from Hancock's similarly club-oriented *Monster* (1980) the following year. "It's really on an exceptional level. He has his own special place. ● "He has a calling... an *anointing*."

Love
Polygone

NORMA JEAN WRIGHT

Norma Jean Wright moved to New York from Ohio in 1976. Within a year, CHIC Organization producers Nile Rodgers and Bernard Edwards featured her as the first lead vocalist of CHIC. Her vocals helped bring "Everybody Dance" to number one on the disco chart for eight consecutive weeks alongside "Dance, Dance, Dance" (featuring Robin Clark and Diva Gray on the verses) from the group's debut album. ● "It happened so fast," she says. "It was just a whirlwind, being out on the road and the fact that the songs took off in such a way that we were working with Chaka Khan and all these people that were superstars to me." ● While CHIC recorded for Atlantic Records, Rodgers and Edwards secured a solo contract for Norma Jean with Albert Grossman's Bearsville Records. The duo continued to hone their style with the singer on her self-titled debut. "Nile and Bernard had a vision of what they wanted, vocally," she says. "They made it clear that the vocals were a part of complementing the rhythm. In some ways they allowed me some freedom. I did have time to play around with the vocals." ● *Norma Jean* (1978) featured material produced expressly for the clubs plus an array of ballads. "It's a *good* album," she says. "Nile and Bernard did a great job. I was very happy with the production. It was a true reflection of me, vocally. I loved all of those songs." "Sorcerer," "I Like Love," the Top 20 R&B hit "Saturday," and her cover of Sam Cooke's "Having a Party" all made the Top 10 of the disco chart. She continued working with the CHIC Organization on her follow-up single, "High Society" (1979), and sang background on *We Are Family* (1979) by Sister Sledge, which continued to establish CHIC's distinct musical imprint. ● "It was a wonderful time," she says. "I'm grateful through it all."

LINDA CLIFFORD

Linda Clifford recalls the day in April 1978 when "If My Friends Could See Me Now" and "Runaway Love" topped *Billboard*'s disco chart. "I got a call from Curtis Mayfield's partner," she says. "I was on my hands and knees washing my kitchen floor. The phone rang. I picked up the phone. He said, 'You're number one in *Billboard.*' I said, 'Very funny' and I hung up. He called back—'Don't hang up. I'm not kidding.' I immediately dropped the phone, ran out, and bought a copy of *Billboard* because I had to see it." ● Produced by Gil Askey, *If My Friends Could See Me Now* (1978) doubled as the title to Clifford's second album for Curtom Records. The Chicago-based vocalist turned the showstopper from *Sweet Charity* into a personal anthem. "I was taken aback by the *fullness* and the beauty of the sound, the *real* musicians playing," she says. "This is beauty of another type from the Broadway show but still beauty just the same. I became so proud of the fact that this was going to be my song. I felt I really have to put everything I have into this. I had no idea that the song affected so many people the way that it affected me. A lot of people could relate to having had something negative in their life at one time and then pulling themselves out." ● Though Clifford returned to number one with "Red Light" from *Fame* (1980) and Isaac Hayes' "Shoot Your Best Shot," her first number one held a special place. "This is the one that really got things rolling for me," she says. "This was my future, my joy. ● "It was my everything because all of the emotions that you can think of were wrapped up in this album."

THE REAL THING

"Yes! You've nailed it. Record of the Week." That's what the BBC told The Real Thing when they played their revised version of "Can You Feel the Force?" Replete with *Star Wars*-inspired sound effects and a surge of crowd noises, the lead single from *Step Into Our World* (1978) gave band members [left to right] Chris Amoo, Eddie Amoo, Dave Smith, and Ray Lake a Top 5 UK smash, selling 49,000 copies in one day and storming clubs across the continent with John Luongo's 12-inch remix. "We were trying to come up with a groove that we could do after 'You to Me Are Everything' as a finale," notes Chris Amoo, who wrote the song with his brother Eddie. "That's how 'Feel the Force,' the rhythm and everything, came about." ● "You to Me Are Everything" was a force unto itself. The Real Thing made history in June 1976 as the first Black British band to top the UK chart when the song spent three weeks at number one. Amoo first glimpsed the song's potential at The Timepiece nightclub in Liverpool. "That's where we played 'You to Me' for the first time," he recalls. "I took it down as a white acetate. My friend Les Spaine was a hugely popular DJ. He put it on and the whole floor just filled up. Les turns to me and says, 'You've got a hit there.'" ● The Real Thing's own compositions reflected their impressive range. "We've always been inspired by American music, *always*, and nothing else," adds Amoo. "There was two sorts of elements coming into The Real Thing. The O'Jays and all them type of bands inspired us to write 'Love's Such a Wonderful Thing' whereas Miles Davis and Donald Byrd were the ones who inspired us to write 'Children of the Ghetto.'" No matter the influence, The Real Thing always made listeners feel the force.

Escort Guide
vice
phone
247731

PATTIE BROOKS

"The moonlight, the music and you," Pattie Brooks sang on "After Dark." Her alluring vocal summoned nocturnal fantasies set against a throbbing, percussive beat. Written and produced by Simon Soussan, "After Dark" was spotlighted in *Thank God It's Friday* (1978) and topped the disco chart in June 1978. ● Only a year earlier, Brooks had been singing with Ann-Margaret in Las Vegas and recording backgrounds for Diana Ross and Donna Summer. "I didn't know anything about disco," she recalls. "'A disco record. Well, what's that?'" Brooks quickly learned. After meeting Soussan in Los Angeles, she signed with Casablanca Records and released her first of four albums for the label, *Love Shook* (1977). ● A cover of Leon Huff's "Girl, Don't Make Me Wait" made the disco Top 5 and introduced Brooks to a whole new scene. "I went to my first disco club. I had no idea what I was getting myself into," she continues. "They had me up on a catwalk and the guy said, 'When we point to you, the spotlight will hit you.' I started singing. There were tons of guys there. They were just in heaven. 'So, *this* is disco!'" ● Brooks' arrival at Casablanca coincided with the label's ascent in the industry. "Neil Bogart had his little empire," she says. "Casablanca was like the number one label. Marc Simon [*Director of Special Projects*] was the boy wonder. He really took me under his wing because they gave him carte blanche with the disco scene. 'After Dark' just took off by itself. They played it at peak time around midnight. People would come back from France and tell me, 'Oh, they're playing it all over the Champs-Élysées.' People were in love with the music. They were in love with each other. It was just a wonderful time."

THE ROLLING STONES

"That particular groove was the groove of the moment," Mick Jagger, speaking to Yahoo Entertainment, said about The Rolling Stones' "Miss You," the lead single off their album *Some Girls* (1978). "You don't really play the grooves of yesteryear when you make records; you play the grooves of now. And that sort of beat was the thing that was going around at the time." ● It was Billy Preston who introduced Jagger to the track's bass drum thump, along with an idea for the bass line. Drummer Charlie Watts and bassist Bill Wyman refined and polished those elements, drawing from their own experience of hearing disco played in the clubs. "At the time, it wasn't necessarily 'disco music' to us," said Keith Richards [pictured on "Miss You" video shoot]. "It was just another rhythm-and-blues beat. No doubt hanging around in bars and clubs a lot had something to do with it." ● Having fashioned their sound from R&B from the very beginning of their career, the band's music had been a presence in New York clubs over the past decade. In fact, DJ Steve D'Acquisto regularly played "Sympathy for the Devil" (1968) at Sanctuary. "To hear the DJ, ensconced in the church's altar, play 'Sympathy for the Devil' was one of the climaxes of the evening," said principal Joffrey Ballet dancer Christian Holder. ● Two years before "Miss You" hit number one on the pop chart in August 1978, *Cash Box* hailed the group's funk-driven "Hot Stuff" as a "hot disco tune, with driving, fleshed-out R&B overtones," while *Emotional Rescue* (1980) kept the grooves going with tracks like "Dance, Pt. 2." However, the "Special Disco Version" of "Miss You" mixed by engineer Bob Clearmountain was a landmark release for The Rolling Stones—it marked the group's first 12-inch single and their first Top 10 disco hit.

CHERYL LYNN

The yellow brick road led to Studio 54 for Cheryl Lynn. In just two years, she'd gone from starring in the national touring company of *The Wiz* to celebrating the success of her number one R&B hit "Got to Be Real," which was featured on the two LP *A Night at Studio 54* (1979) collection. It was there where the young singer danced with the Godfather of Soul himself. "I started to dance and James Brown saw me on the dance floor," Cheryl Lynn recalls. "He ran to the floor to dance with me, doing all of his little steps. The whole crowd circled around us watching us dance at Studio 54!" ● Just a year earlier, Cheryl Lynn had fielded offers from several major record companies, but chose CBS Records after meeting CEO Walter Yetnikoff and president Bruce Lundvall. Toto member David Paich and his father Marty Paich produced her self-titled debut, which included a few of the singer's own songwriting contributions. "We would be in the garage at David's dad's house," she recalls. "That's where he set up all his music equipment. He'd start playing and I'd start singing. He came up with the music and I came up with the hook for 'Got to Be Real.' I was just saying what I felt. That's how the words came about. I thought about people being true to each other, a relationship working when you're honest and being real with a person." ● Cheryl Lynn's remarkable range reached a whole other galaxy on the thrilling cosmic ride of "Star Love." Recording the song with Paich and the musicians was "like a rocket shooting up," she says. "We were up in the stars and the *moon*! The next thing I know I'm hitting the notes, going out of this world! That was the number one song I had to sing at the clubs." The stars not only shined for Cheryl Lynn; they blazed.

"For me, disco was very liberating," said Musique founder Patrick Adams. "I could be as adventurous as I wanted to be." The New York-based producer, songwriter, and arranger was the force behind several studio projects, including Phreek, Universal Robot Band, Poussez, and Inner Life, but it was his production for Musique's *Keep on Jumpin'* that brought him to the top of the disco charts for the first time in September 1978. "The recordings for Cloud One and Bumblebee Unlimited allowed me to explore uncharted territory," he adds. "Musique let me go with full orchestra." ● Adams enlisted some of New York's most prolific session vocalists for the album, including Jocelyn Brown and Christine Wiltshire [left]. "Patrick and Christine created the sound of Musique," says Mary Seymour [center]. "It was just supposed to be a studio project. Then once it became so successful, Christine called me and said, 'We need a group.'" Wiltshire, Seymour, and Gina Taylor [right] fronted Musique as "Keep on Jumpin'" and "In the Bush" took off in the clubs. The trio toured everywhere from Venezuela to Singapore, while dancers across the US chanted along to the group's hits. "In the Bush" was even featured on *A Night at Studio 54* (1979). ● "With that lineup, we worked five nights a week," adds Seymour. "You could play three clubs a night if you wanted to. We were so big that, in 1979, Sylvester opened for us! A lot of the style from Musique was very staccato. Therefore, it's not as much singing as talking in pitch. To me, there was a very classical element in Patrick's arranging. He knew how to mix what was required and still give the elements of authenticity for what *he* was writing. He had horn lines and violin lines that are just from the sky!" From the sky to the dance floor, Musique got everybody jumpin'.

VOYAGE

Voyage was French disco at its finest. ● Paris-based Marc Chantereau (keyboards), Pierre Alain Dahan (drums), and Slim Pezin (guitar) formed Voyage after playing on sessions for Cerrone, Alec R. Costandinos, Crystal Grass, Don Ray, and Santa Esmeralda. "We were working on all records of all French singers, in studios all day long and on stage in the evening," says Chantereau [front]. "We were well-known for that. They called us the 'sharks of the studios.'" ● The trio took disco revelers along for the ride on *Voyage* (1977). "We started brainstorming," he recalls. "We said we'll do a voyage around the world with different music, always with the bass drum. We went to London and wrote the arrangement of brass in the hotel! We recorded the album in four days." Chantereau penned the main melody line for the album's exquisite opener "From East to West," featuring vocalists Kay Garner and Stephanie De-Sykes. The album proceeded with adventures in Africa, Asia, Europe, and South America. ● France was the first place to hear Voyage. "Élysée Matignon was a nightclub in Paris," says Chantereau. "The DJ was the brother of Grace Jones—Christian Joes. He heard the music and said, 'I love it! Give me a few records.' One week later, he went to Regine's in New York City and gave the record to the DJ." Meanwhile, executive producer Roger Tokarz brought the album to MIDEM in Cannes where T.K. Records signed the group. Voyage topped the disco chart for three weeks in April 1978. "It was incredible to do a record and that it was a success in the USA," says Chantereau. ● Voyage returned to number one with *Fly Away* (1978), featuring vocalist Sylvia Mason-James [*center*] on the album's ebullient title track, while Kay Garner and Stephanie De-Sykes shaped "Souvenirs" with one of the era's dreamiest vocal blends. Travelers of all dance persuasions joined Voyage, once again, for an unforgettable disco fantasy that spanned the globe. No baggage necessary.

SANTA ESMERALDA

How did a fusion of flamenco and disco reinvent "Don't Let Me Be Misunderstood" more than a decade after it became a signature tune for both Nina Simone and The Animals? ● Santa Esmeralda vocalist Leroy Gómez helped give the song a whole new life. French producers Nicolas Skorsky and Jean-Manuel de Scarano contracted Gómez, plus Cerrone arranger Don Ray, and a cadre of Paris-based musicians to recast the song for the discothèques. "It was a magical thing that happened over a four-five-day period in the studio with a bunch of guys having fun," says Gómez [second from left]. "These are all guys I was doing studio work with. We had no idea it was going to be what it turned out to be." Voyage writer and producer Marc Chantereau was among the musicians on the track. "The introduction was made by me, with my wife's shoes, like it was a real Spanish dance," he notes. ● Gómez made frequent appearances with a trio of dancers, including his wife Tequila [left], as "Don't Let Me Be Misunderstood" reached number one in Germany and made the Top 5 of the disco chart in 1977. He went solo with *Gypsy Woman* (1978) and *I Got It Bad* (1979) while Santa Esmeralda producers hired vocalist Jimmy Goings and scored additional club hits like "The House of the Rising Sun" and "Another Cha-Cha." ● Casablanca Records was home base for both Santa Esmeralda and Gómez's solo projects, continuing its reign as disco's leading record company. "'Don't Let Me Be Misunderstood' was 17 minutes and that was done because of what Giorgio Moroder and Donna Summer did with 'Love to Love You Baby,'" notes Gómez. "That would never have happened if Casablanca hadn't taken the idea of the 17-minute mix. It brought a whole new aspect to the dance scene."

Lido Musique
SANTA ESMERALDA
Don't let me be misunderstood
Leroy Gomez

TERI DeSARIO

Coconut Grove, 1977. Teri DeSario and her band are performing at the Village Inn. Bee Gees producer Albhy Galuten stops by the club, about 20 miles south from Criteria Recording Studio in Miami where Barry Gibb and his brothers recorded *Main Course* (1975) and *Children of the World* (1976). He approaches DeSario after the set. ● "He said that Barry was looking to do a project," she recalls. "This is when I think he was just beginning to think about producing other people. I made a demo and I guess Barry liked it. I came in and I got to choose between three songs. It was either 'Ain't Nothing Gonna Keep Me From You,' 'Emotion,' or another song that Andy Gibb ended up doing." DeSario chose Gibb's self-penned "Ain't Nothing Gonna Keep Me From You." "It's a *beautiful* song," she says. "It could be about someone who sees who you really are, or a friend who will never desert you, or a lover who will be with you though thick and thin. ● "Barry's a *great* songwriter. I'm a soprano but he did all the high parts. Barry taught me a very important lesson about how to record. He said it's going to be the emphasis of the words on particular beats—'I admit it. I'm *really* a *dreamer*.' You have to be out front in terms of emphasizing the rhythmic aspects in the consonants." ● Neil Bogart heard DeSario's recording and signed her to Casablanca Records where she recorded three albums for the label. Producers Ron and Howard Albert helmed her debut, *Pleasure Train* (1978), at the legendary Muscle Shoals Studio in Alabama. However, it was a remixed and extended version of Gibb's song that brought DeSario's voice to the discothèques, especially Paradise Garage where Larry Levan regularly included the song in his set. Nothing could keep Teri DeSario from enchanting dancers with a timeless performance.

BROOKLYN DREAMS

Brooklyn Dreams brought the street corner harmonies of Flatbush to Los Angeles. Group members Bruce Sudano, Joe "Bean" Esposito, and Eddie Hokenson had known each other as teenagers, forging a bond that outlived multiple groups before relocating to the west coast in 1976. "There was some sort of thing that happened when the three of us got together," says Esposito. "It transcended the music." ● The trio also knew the liberating power of dance. "If it helps you find your freedom, how could it steer you wrong?" they sang on "Street Dance" off their self-titled debut for Millennium Records. DJ Bobby Guttadaro remixed the track along with the group's "Music, Harmony and Rhythm," introducing Brooklyn Dreams to a whole new audience in the discothèques. ● Moving to Millennium's distributor, Casablanca Records, Brooklyn Dreams tailored *Sleepless Nights* (1979) and *Joy Ride* (1979) specifically for the discos, especially after joining Donna Summer on "Heaven Knows" from her *Live & More* (1978) album. Esposito shared the duet with Summer, which made the Top 5 in January 1979. "They asked me to do it," he says. "It was really like an afterthought. We did it in one or two takes. Neil Bogart heard it and said, 'That's a hit song. Let's edit that and put that out.'" ● Brooklyn Dreams also co-wrote "Bad Girls" with Summer, celebrating a number one hit on the pop, R&B, and disco charts. It capped a period of non-stop recording and touring, plus appearances in *American Hot Wax* (1978) and songwriting contributions for *Thank God it's Friday* (1978), *Foxes* (1980), and *Hollywood Knights* (1980). "Brooklyn Dreams was a powerful entity," says Sudano. "Every day was another TV show, another recording session, or another movie. There was a constant flow. ● "We were just on fire."

MELBA MOORE

In between her Tony Award-winning performance in *Purlie* (1970) and her historic solo show at The Metropolitan Opera House in 1976, Melba Moore became a sensation in the discos. Produced by Van McCoy, *This Is It* (1976) brought her to the disco Top 10 for the first time. "Van McCoy had a universal feel," she says. "His background is very similar in some ways to Philly International. It's very classy and it allows a variety of styles and feels to accommodate it." ● Moore found her greatest club success with "You Stepped Into My Life," an album track from the Bee Gees' *Children of the World* (1976) that McFadden & Whitehead produced on her first LP for Epic Records, *Melba* (1978). "My management was looking at the Gibbs' catalog of music," she says, "They were having hit after hit after hit. We thought, 'They're on a roll. Why don't we get on *their* bandwagon!' McFadden & Whitehead liked the song and they felt they could do something with it." ● John Luongo's remix of "You Stepped Into My Life" shot to #5 on the disco chart, followed by "Pick Me Up, I'll Dance," a sweeping track written and produced by McFadden & Whitehead. "That feel is really John Whitehead," Moore notes about the latter tune. "He had those beautiful, romantic-sounding chords. I wanted to have a very tall handsome young man doing a ballroom disco dance with me, like one of those romantic musical movies with Cyd Charisse." ● After teaming with producer Pete Bellotte on *Burn* (1979), Moore remained active in the clubs over the next four decades. "You need joy, you need energy, so dance music in some form or another is always gonna be here," she says. "We think that because it's so joyful, it's frivolous, but joy is not frivolous. It's your survival."

How did Foxy get to number one? By getting kicked out of a club. ● The Miami-based band had minor success in the discos before "Get Off" propelled Ish Ledesma (lead vocals and guitar), Richie Puente (percussion), Joe Galdo (drums), Arnold Paseiro (bass), and Charlie Murciano (keyboards) to the top in the summer of 1978. "We did a gig in Ocean City, Maryland," recalls Ledesma [top center]. "We did the 'oo-ah oo-ah' thing. It was in vogue to do that, but the owner of the club hated it. At the end of the night, he came up to me: 'If you guys do that 'oo-ah oo-ah' shit one more time, I'm gonna choke your asses and throw you into the bay.'" That same night, Ledesma wrote "Get Off," building the hook around *four* sets of "oo-ah oo-ah's." ● "The next day, we went to the club and rehearsed it without doing the 'oo-ah's,'" he continues. "Then, at night on the second set, I said 'Let's do it.' We didn't even get through the first set of 'oo-ah's' before the bouncers came onstage, unplugged us, and threw us out of the club." ● T.K. Records president Henry Stone had an altogether different response to what became the title of Foxy's second album. Ledesma continues, "I told Henry, 'We started playing this song that I wrote. The owner hated it so much that he kicked us out of the club... so there's *got* to be something there!' Henry heard it: 'This is a number one smash!' In four weeks, it was number one on the R&B chart." ● The tight yet supercharged disco-funk of "Get Off" signaled the direction for Foxy's third album. "We didn't really hit our stride until *Hot Numbers* (1979)," says Ledesma. "It was the only album that was consistent with a sound and an attitude. We weren't fishing for styles." Whether it was "Get Off" or "Hot Number," Foxy sizzled with every groove.

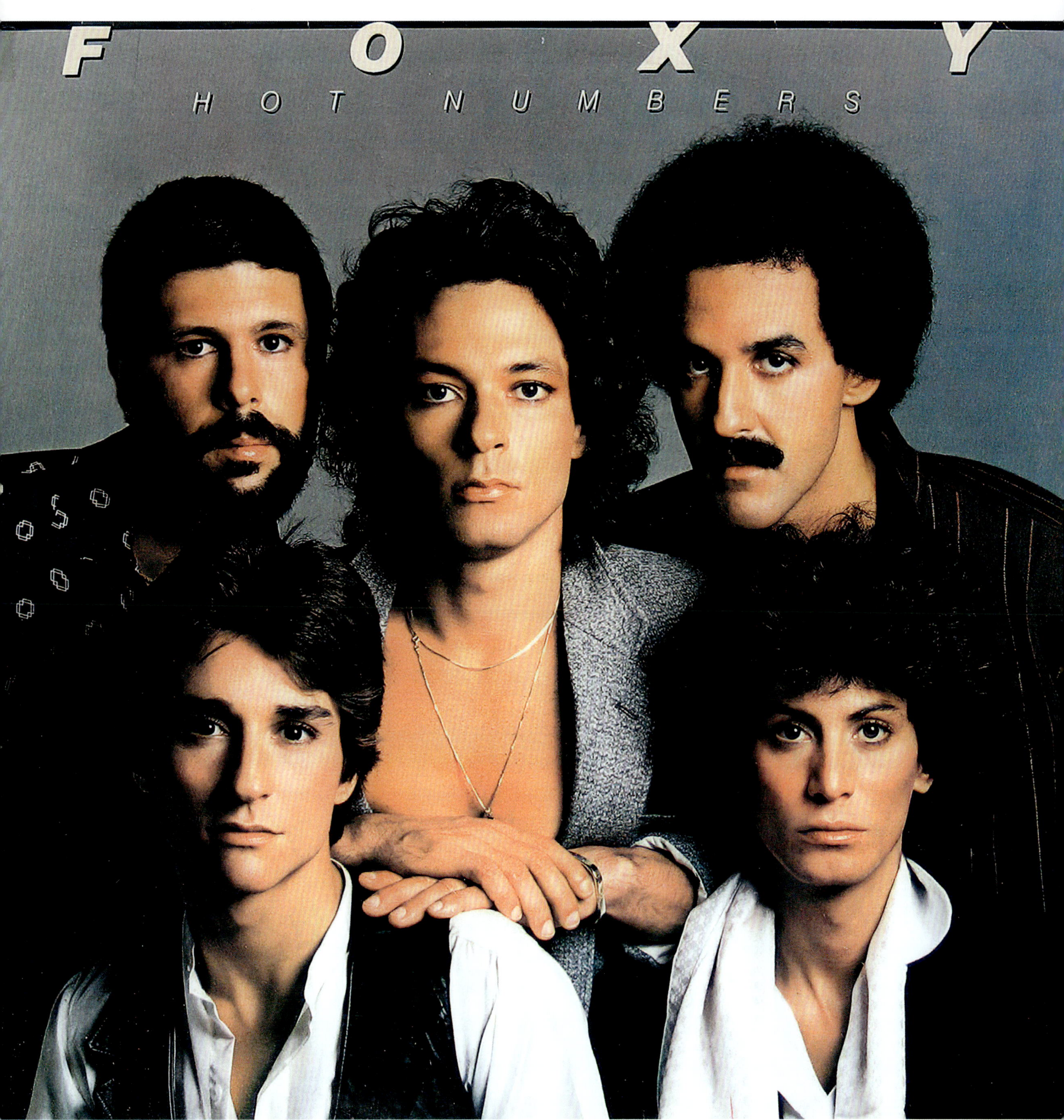
F O X Y
H O T N U M B E R S

ROD STEWART

"Can Rock and Music Coexist?" *The New York Times* asked in January 1979. A photo of Rod Stewart furnished the answer. His unabashed nod to disco gave the British rocker one of the most successful singles of his career. ● "I had been listening to records by CHIC, where the bass guitar is the driving force and almost the main providers of the melody," he wrote years later in his autobiography. "I had also been listening a lot to 'Native New Yorker' by Odyssey, a track I loved. And there was the Stones' 'Miss You': a rock band's take on disco, a blend that really appealed to me. And so the question was 'Can we come up with something along the lines of that?' And what emerged was a song called 'Da Ya Think I'm Sexy?'" ● Stewart collaborated with Duane Hitchings and former Vanilla Fudge drummer Carmine Appice on the song, repurposing the hook from Brazilian artist Jorge Ben Jor's "Taj Mahal" for the chorus, plus a string line from Bobby Womack's "(If You Want My Love) Put Something Down On It." Though the spandex-clad singer certainly fit the part, he was quick to clarify the song's third person storyline. "It wasn't *me* asking every Tom, Dick, and Harriet in the world if they thought *I* was sexy," he said. "There was a story being told here." ● "Da Ya Think I'm Sexy?" topped the pop and disco charts and sold more than two million copies in North America. Donna Summer was among the record's many admirers. "I think that Rod Stewart did a good job of assimilating the whole genre and saying, 'Hey man, I'm a rock guy but I like to dance. It's cool,'" she said. From the singer's seductive rasp to Phil Chen's sinewy bass line, all the elements coalesced into a sumptuously produced disco classic.

McFADDEN & WHITEHEAD

Listeners knew McFadden & Whitehead's music before they knew their names. As staff writers for Kenny Gamble and Leon Huff's Philadelphia International Records, Gene McFadden and John Whitehead penned some of the biggest hits recorded by the label's artists, including The O'Jays ("Back Stabbers"), The Intruders ("I'll Always Love My Mama"), Harold Melvin & the Blue Notes ("Bad Luck"), Archie Bell & the Drells ("Let's Groove"), and Teddy Pendergrass ("The More I Get, The More I Want"). They also produced two albums for Melba Moore, *A Portrait of Melba* (1977) and *Melba* (1978), which featured her hit rendition of the Bee Gees' "You Stepped Into My Life" and the duo's own "Pick Me Up, I'll Dance." ● "They were a comedy team," says Moore. "They were funny about everything. They really were committed to their music. Normally, you would say they were serious about their music, but they weren't serious about *anything*! John had more to do with melody and lyric and Gene had more to do with the actual arrangement, especially the feel and the mood of the rhythm. He could hear what the drum should be, he could hear what the bass line should be, and he really knew exactly what the strings should do. He wasn't a trained musician. He didn't know how to read music, but he could hear and see everything, what each instrument should do." ● Having previously recorded for Gamble and Huff's TSOP imprint with their group Talk of the Town, McFadden & Whitehead debuted in 1979 with their first album as a duo. They topped the R&B chart with a showstopping club anthem that earned them a GRAMMY nomination and also defined their career trajectory: "Ain't No Stopping' Us Now." Don Cornelius described McFadden & Whitehead best when they appeared on *Soul Train*: "Two brilliant composers... one of the hottest performing acts in the business."

EVELYN "CHAMPAGNE" KING

When Evelyn "Champagne" King stepped onstage with Linda Clifford to present Isaac Hayes with an American Music Award for "Favorite Disco Male Artist" in January 1979, she was also celebrating her own AMA nomination that evening for her debut single "Shame." King had recorded the song two years earlier for her RCA Records debut, the gold-selling *Smooth Talk* (1977) produced by T. Life. ● Almost overnight, she'd gone from singing "A Change is Gonna Come" a cappella in the halls of Sigma Sound Studios to recording a Top 10 classic of the disco era. "T. Life was this tall, thin man walking up to me talking about he's going to make me a star," recalls King, whose "bubbly" personality inspired her stage name. "I had no clue who he was. He talked to my mom and my dad. I remember when we were all together—the songwriters John Fitch and Reuben Cross, T. Life, and my dad—and we were listening to 'Shame.' He said, 'Sing it down. Show me what you got.' They started strumming on a guitar and I just sang it. 'This is a hit!' ● "As far as I know, my dad and T. Life would send tapes to Gamble and Huff at Philly International. T. Life would always say, 'You gotta hear this young girl.' I was 15. It wasn't the time for me, as far as they were concerned. As far as RCA and T. Life were concerned, it didn't matter." ● Featuring Instant Funk as the backing band, both "Shame" and "I Don't Know If It's Right" gave the singer a pair of gold records, especially after Al Garrison and Ice Palace DJ David Todd remixed the former song for the clubs. The young King was suddenly a disco queen.

CHIC. One word. Boundless inspiration. ● From the moment "Everybody Dance" and "Dance, Dance, Dance (Yowsah, Yowsah Yowsah)" galloped to number one for eight weeks in 1977, CHIC's influence was undeniable. CHIC Organization producers Nile Rodgers (guitar) [left] and Bernard Edwards (bass) [second from left] drew on elements of jazz, funk, R&B, and classical to create their own realm of dance music, featuring drummer Tony Thompson [second from right], the CHIC Strings, plus vocalists Luther Vandross, Robin Clark, Diva Gray, David Lasley, Norma Jean Wright, and Alfa Anderson on the band's self-titled debut. ● "The element of surprise for ourselves, improvising, was an exciting part of music," says Rodgers. "We loved writing in the studio. Our best attributes were directing people on the spot. That's the environment we excelled in." Adding vocalist Luci Martin [center] to the lineup on *C'est CHIC* (1978), the band scored number one pop anthems like "Le Freak" and recorded sublime tracks like "I Want Your Love," which spotlighted Alfa Anderson [right] on lead. ● Fonzi Thornton and Michelle Cobbs rounded out CHIC's vocal sound, beginning with *Risqué* (1979). "When it was time to do the lead for 'Good Times' and 'My Forbidden Lover,' Bernard and Nile called me up and said, 'We want you to come to the studio to sing the group lead with Alfa and Luci,'" says Thornton. "People don't realize that there was a man's voice singing with Alfa and Luci because my voice blends so well with female voices. Alfa, Luci, Michelle, and I actually became the CHIC vocal group and *that's* the sound that you hear on all their records from *Risqué* on, including Diana Ross' *diana* (1980) album." ● Decades after the CHIC Organization produced career-defining hits for Diana Ross ("I'm Coming Out") and Sister Sledge ("We Are Family"), the Library of Congress added "Le Freak" to the National Recording Registry in 2017. Then and now, it furnishes the disco era's most coveted invitation: "Just come on down to 54."

BLONDIE

Midtown Manhattan's New York, New York discothèque showcased Blondie in full disco splendor. Draped in a diaphanous ensemble designed by Stephen Sprouse, lead vocalist Debbie Harry radiated luminescent glamour during the video shoot for "Heart of Glass" [pictured], the group's first of four chart-topping pop hits. The club's swirling lights and flashes of jagged lightning bolts moved in sync with the song's percolating groove. ● Harry and guitarist Chris Stein had tried different ideas for "Heart of Glass," which had an earlier incarnation as "The Disco Song," before sharing it with producer Mike Chapman during the sessions for *Parallel Lines* (1978). "He was like a sieve or focal point," says Harry. "He would take all of the material from the Blondie writers and put it all together and focus it and make it cohesive." ● Chapman's precision gave "Heart of Glass" a crystalline sheen that enveloped Harry's voice to shimmering effect. "The thing that I loved about Debbie is that she always convinced me of her songs," says CHIC producer Nile Rodgers. "When I listened to Blondie, I *believed* the role that she was playing." Her chameleonic vocal approach and strong visual identity distinguished Blondie from other bands who emerged out of New York's punk and art scene. "I think that's one of the most valuable things that any of us can have: to find, truly, what is your unique voice," she says. ● During the summer of 1979, Harry collaborated with Giorgio Moroder on "Call Me," the theme to *American Gigolo* (1980) that would bring Blondie back to number one, plus #2 on the disco chart. "'Call Me' is a masterpiece," says Harold Faltermeyer, who arranged the song and played synthesizer on the track. "It's another genius Giorgio Moroder melody. 'He speaks the languages of love'—this was Deborah Harry's idea. It's one of the best movie songs of that time." And for the clubs? A hybrid of dance and rock that set a thrilling tone for the new decade.

PARLIAMENT-FUNKADELIC

Parliament landed at Madison Square Garden in February 1979. A few months earlier, they'd released *Motor Booty Affair* (1978), their seventh LP for Casablanca Records, "a concept album about raising Atlantis in the name of the funk." The album introduced new characters like Mr. Wiggles and spawned the chart-topping "Aqua Boogie (A Psychoalphadiscobetabioaquadoloop)," which continued the adventures of Sir Nose D'Voidoffunk. The tour was Parliament's most theatrical yet. "We were fully into the Broadway mentality. We had fish costumes for everyone in the band," George Clinton, who adorned himself with glittering scales, later wrote in his autobiography. ● The P-Funk collective had a following that could fill stadiums, but it was in the clubs where their music flourished. Casablanca included the group's "Up for the Down Stroke" and "Give Up the Funk (Tear the Roof Off the Sucker)" on the label's *Get Down and Boogie* (1976) compilation featuring label mates Donna Summer and Giorgio Moroder. In fact, album coordinator DJ Bobby Guttadaro had made the latter tune a staple at Infinity in downtown Manhattan upon the song's release on Parliament's *Mothership Connection* (1975). Similarly, "Flash Light" and "Bop Gun"—"a weapon that thwarted any resistance to the funk"—jumped from *Funkentelechy vs. the Placebo Syndrome* (1977) into the discos, further illustrating how clubs embraced Parliament's animated universe. ● "The revolution we had in mind was peaceful, hedonistic, and prone to winking at itself in the mirror," wrote Clinton. "A record can overturn just by turning, can bring about revolution just by revolving." Indeed, the Funkadelic side of his organization on Warner Bros. sparked a club anthem with the title track to *One Nation Under a Groove* (1978), topping the R&B chart for six weeks while other acts like Parlet, Bootsy's Rubber Band, The Brides of Funkenstein, and arranger and multi-instrumentalist Bernie Worrell branched out from the P-Funk collective with their own grooves. ● To quote Worrell himself, "P-Funk was wild, man."

INSTANT FUNK

"Music has a life, it has a pulse," says Instant Funk co-founder and guitarist Kym Miller. "You tap into the life of the music, then you're tapping into every rhythmic sphere that moves everybody." Whether backing South Shore Commission on the number one disco hit "Free Man" (1975), playing on Evelyn "Champagne" King's debut "Shame" (1977), or recording their own material, Instant Funk mastered the talent of making people move. It even inspired the band's name: "Our manager, Leroy Ellis, used to say that we can come up with tunes at the drop of the dime," says co-founder and bassist Raymond Earl [front row, second from right]. ● The Trenton, NJ-based group found a home in Philadelphia at Sigma Sound Studios, recording with producers like Bunny Sigler, T. Life, and Norman Harris. Released on Gamble and Huff's TSOP label, *Get Down with the Philly Jump* (1976) spawned the Top 40 club hit "It Ain't Reggae (But It's Funky)," and introduced the band's unique amalgamation of grooves. ● After relocating to Salsoul Records, Instant Funk recorded one of the era's most enticing classics, "I Got My Mind Made Up (You Can Get It Girl)." "My brother Scotty [front row, second from left] and his friend were on the porch, singing this hook, but they didn't have any music," recalls Miller [second row, middle]. "As I'm coming up the steps, this guitar scratch just came in my head, so I snapped the guitar from Scotty and I just started playing." Raymond Earl rounded out Miller's groove with a delectable bass line. "I heard something like The Blackbyrds' 'Rock Creek Park,'" he says. "I was in that frame of mind." ● When Salsoul enlisted Paradise Garage DJ Larry Levan to remix "I Got My Mind Made Up," the track topped the disco chart in March 1979. "This record took off so fast, it caught us off guard," says Miller. Instant Funk had found instant success.

sigma sound studios
PHILADELPHIA • NEW YORK

AMII STEWART

"I can remember dancing all night," Amii Stewart recalls. It was the mid-1970s and she was working on the hit Broadway revue *Bubbling Brown Sugar.* "You do the matinee, go home, you hit the club Sunday night. Walk out of the club and the sun's coming up. We would have fried chicken and waffles. I would go home and sleep all day, because theaters are dark on Monday, and be back in the theater on Tuesday." ● Stewart's own voice was about to keep dancers on the floor all night long. ● Producer Barry Leng met Stewart backstage after she moved to London to star in the West End production of *Bubbling Brown Sugar.* He invited her to record a demo, "You Really Touched My Heart," while the singer signed with Hansa International, a German company that achieved success throughout Europe with disco acts like Boney M. and Eruption and would release Stewart's first three albums. ● Leng transformed "Knock on Wood"—a Memphis soul classic by Eddie Floyd—into an explosive, platinum-selling disco workout. "It was one of Barry's favorite songs," says Stewart, whose version topped the Hot 100 in April 1979 and garnered a GRAMMY nomination. "How he came up with that arrangement, I will never know!" ● "When I cut 'Knock on Wood,' I never stopped doing *Bubbling Brown Sugar,"* she continues. "I'm coming from Ellington and the theater, and I thought that song was gonna do nothing. I am not giving up my day job! The head of the record company [Trudy Meisel] had to come to the theater and say, 'Amii, we have to talk. You have to leave the show.' 'I have to *leave*?' 'Yes. You've got promotion, you've got TV.' It just hit in every country, every month! Eddie Floyd got in touch with me and said, 'Any more songs of mine you wanna do?'" [*laughs*] ● Stewart would subsequently establish a successful career in Italy, performing for Italian president Sergio Mattarella in 2024. As a formidable vocal force, Stewart's own crown shines as majestically as ever.

BONNIE POINTER

Bonnie Pointer was the first member of The Pointer Sisters to venture solo. "She left in 1976, but she was the favorite, from what I recall," says Ruth Pointer. "We always called her our Beyoncé. She was a very flamboyant, outspoken, and lovable bundle of joy. People always gravitated towards her." ● After establishing the group with hits like "Yes We Can Can," "How Long (Betcha Got a Chick on the Side)," and the GRAMMY-winning country song "Fairytale," Bonnie launched her solo career in 1978. "I just wanted to find and learn about Bonnie," she told *JET* magazine. "I wanted to know what she was about, without any help from anyone else. I wanted to know what I could do on my own, what my limitations were and how much I had grown." ● Pointer signed with Motown Records, releasing a pair of self-titled albums in 1978 and 1979 helmed by staff producer (and future husband) Jeffrey Bowen. Pointer's first solo hit, "Free Me From My Freedom/ Tie Me to a Tree (Handcuff Me)," immediately caused a sensation with its suggestive title. "I wrote the part that's causing all the controversy—'tie me to a tree, handcuff me,'" she explained at the time. "I just said what I felt the song is saying. I had some feedback from people on the radio who wouldn't play it. They think I'm being masochistic or something, but I'm seeing a wholly different story." ● During the summer of 1979, Pointer triumphed on the charts with a glossy, pop-disco rendition of The Elgins' "Heaven Must Have Sent You," using the beat from Village People's "Y.M.C.A." as inspiration. She followed up with a similar take on The Four Tops' "I Can't Help Myself," recasting Motown classics for the disco era with her own distinctive style. In remembering her sister years later, Ruth Pointer put it best: "Bonnie was like a ball of fire."

"Dancing Queen" is the crowning jewel in ABBA's catalog. "I knew it was absolutely the best song ABBA had ever done," said Anni-Frid Lyngstad in an interview with *The Guardian*. "And that was before me and Agnetha had even sung on it!" ● "Dancing Queen" shot from the group's *Arrival* (1976) album to number one in more than a dozen countries, including the US, UK, and the group's home base, Sweden. Rhythmically, the song owed its shuffling bounce to Miami sunshine: George McCrae's "Rock Your Baby" had inspired Benny Andersson and Björn Ulvaeus as they developed the track. Though ABBA had always been oriented towards radio, "Dancing Queen" marked the group's venture towards dance music. They even filmed the music video at Alexandra's, a popular discothèque in Stockholm. ● Sleekly attired in posh club wear, ABBA returned to Alexandra's a few years later to photograph the cover of *Voulez-Vous* (1979). The album's release was bookended by two singles that reflected ABBA's mastery of pop-disco elements, "Summer Night City" and "Gimme! Gimme! Gimme! (A Man After Midnight)." Whereas the Miami sound had influenced "Dancing Queen" from afar, the rhythm track to "Voulez-Vous" was actually cut at Criteria Studios in Miami where the Bee Gees recorded at the time. ● Listening to American Top 40 radio during a visit to the Bahamas in January 1979 had jumpstarted ABBA's ideas for the album. "We were influenced by everything we heard, everything that was around us, such as The Bee Gees, Donna Summer, CHIC," Ulvaeus recalled. Recorded with members of the group Foxy, who'd just scored a major club hit with "Get Off," the title song to *Voulez-Vous* signified a rare occasion where ABBA cut a track outside of Sweden. ● "What I had in mind before I even had the title was a kind of nightclub scene, with a certain amount of sexual tension and eyes looking at each other," Ulvaeus said. "I only had to describe that room and what might be happening and then add that final touch: Voulez-Vous?"

moog

SISTER SLEDGE

"We Are Family" was a worldwide anthem. And it almost didn't happen. ● "What people don't know is right before 'We Are Family,' I was ready to say I've had it," recalls lead vocalist Kathy Sledge [top left]. "For nine years, I was singing and doing clubs up and down the turnpike. By the time 'We Are Family' came out, we'd sacrificed so many things, from being on the track team to proms." ● While still attending high school, Kathy, Joni, Kim, and Debbie Sledge became a club draw after signing with Atco Records. "Mama Never Told Me" (1973) and the *Circle of Love* (1975) album were early favorites before CHIC Organization producers Nile Rodgers and Bernard Edwards helmed the Philadelphia-based group's third album, *We Are Family* (1979). Kathy and her sisters inspired every word of the title track. ● "I'm always proud to say that song was literally written about us," says Kathy. "The then record company president Jerry Greenberg was describing us to Bernard and Nile. 'You got to meet these girls. They're family. They flock together like birds of a feather whenever they're up at the label.' Nile and Bernard took out their pens and they started taking notes. That really is a portrait of who we were growing up." ● *We Are Family* topped the R&B albums chart for seven weeks, bolstered by additional cuts like "He's the Greatest Dancer," "Lost in Music," and "Thinking of You." It changed everything for Sister Sledge. "Our first major tour after the record really broke in the country was with the Jacksons," says Kathy. "I was scared to death because I felt like it's not like the small intimate clubs where we're one on one. It's massive crowds. Are they going to like us? What I learned is they loved you even more. ● "Having a hit was just the icing on the cake."

CHER

"I want you to write a song like 'Last Dance.'" ● That was Neil Bogart's mandate for songwriter and producer Bob Esty, who'd been invited to produce Cher for Casablanca Records. Esty had arranged Donna Summer's Oscar-winning standard and knew how to turn a romantic narrative into a dazzling disco wonderland. And that's exactly what he created for Cher. ● "Michele Aller and I got together, and we wrote 'Take Me Home' based on Cher's personality," Esty recalled. "It was from a strong woman's point of view, and it was done in a way that had a melody. We went in to record it. I'd done the guide vocal. We had a rapport and that worked out good. It was a great experience for me because I liked her and I think she liked me at the time." ● Capitalizing on the latest disco trend, Casablanca's New York office held a roller disco party at Empire Rollerdrome in Brooklyn to launch *Take Me Home* (1979). Such promotional efforts paid off. "Take Me Home" made the Top 10 and became Cher's biggest single in five years. She also became one of the celebrity faces of roller disco mania. Her second collaboration with Bob Esty for Casablanca, *Prisoner* (1979), included the rollerskating anthem, "Hell on Wheels." The song's refrain—"Roll on!"—even framed the opening sequence to the film *Roller Boogie* (1979). ● Aside from her collaboration with Giorgio Moroder on the song "Bad Love" for the soundtrack to *Foxes* (1980), Cher's albums were virtually devoid of dance music for two decades until "Believe" completely regenerated her career in 1999. "'Believe' and everything else from then on is based on the 'Take Me Home' experience," Esty noted. And the disco ball has been spinning for Cher ever since.

ANITA WARD

Anita Ward debuted as a bonafide hitmaker. "You'd think she was a Bee Gee from the way her record has been streaking up the charts," *Billboard* marveled in June 1979. Success was swift for the Memphis-based singer. "Ring My Bell" had already topped the disco chart a month earlier and was on its way to hold the number one spot on the pop and R&B charts, simultaneously. ● Barely a year had passed since Ward graduated from Rust College in Jackson, Mississippi, where she sang in the school choir as well as a female gospel group. She met songwriter and producer Frederick Knight, who scored a Top 40 hit on Stax Records in 1972 with "I've Been Lonely for So Long." Recorded at Malaco Studios in Jackson, *Songs of Love* (1979) featured a variety of material to showcase Ward's range. In fact, Knight had originally considered "Ring My Bell" for teenage vocalist Stacy Lattisaw but rewrote it for Ward to furnish the album with another uptempo number. ● Knight's Juana Records released *Songs of Love* via T.K. Records, then at the peak of its powers. "I had started doing substitute teaching while we were waiting to see if the music was going to take off," Ward recalls. "I didn't have to wait very long. I subbed for four months and then 'Ring My Bell' went gold after two weeks. My manager called and said they wanted me to do *The Midnight Special* with Wolfman Jack. They flew in a dancer and others, including a guy from New York to vigorously work with me, showing me how to dance with parts of my body I didn't even know I had." ● "Ring My Bell" topped the chart everywhere from the UK to Spain to New Zealand. Indeed, Anita Ward got bells ringing all over the world.

FRANCE JOLI

"Beach" was the first dance party of its kind in Fire Island Pines... and France Joli was its most radiant star. "My first American performance in front of 5,000 gay men. I have goosebumps every time I talk about it because it's so beautiful and so magical," she says. "It's divine. It's because of them that I'm here." ● The 16-year-old French Canadian vocalist's "Come to Me" was already a hit in Fire Island clubs when she was invited to perform at the event in July 1979, a benefit to raise money for the beachfront community's fire department. "It was like a fairy tale," she says. "All of a sudden, I was Cinderella. I just glided on stage. I remember the spotlight being on me and the wind blowing in my hair. I was trying to give this audience the best of me. Every time I would make a sexy move, they would go nuts." ● Songwriter and producer Tony Green had written "Come to Me" specifically for Joli after hearing the young vocalist sing Barbra Streisand and Olivia Newton-John. "It's a pure romance song," she says. "It suited me so well because I love power ballads. Tony went with 'Come to Me' to MIDEM, which is a convention in Cannes, and he visited all the record companies. There was a big buzz about 'Come to Me' but we went with a small record label because we didn't want to get lost in the shuffle." ● Joli released her self-titled debut on Prelude Records while "Come to Me" crowned the disco chart for three weeks in September 1979. "They pushed the record everywhere," she says. "It started in New York, then countries all over the world picked it up." The glittering kingdom of disco now welcomed a new princess to the party.

A discothèque sealed GQ's destiny. The Bronx-based band had been playing New York for nearly 10 years, including an earlier incarnation as the Rhythm Makers, before taking clubs by storm as GQ ("Good Quality"). Their chart-topping future was months within reach when Arista Records senior vice president Larkin Arnold auditioned the band at Starship Discovery 1. ● "That was an after-hours club we used to play," says guitarist and lead vocalist Emanuel Rahiem LeBlanc (aka "Mr Q"). "It was right behind Port Authority on 42nd Street. The club was at least 5,000 people on four floors. The place opened up at midnight. We had maybe a six or seven o'clock sound check. I remember Larkin Arnold coming with [*manager*] Tony Lopez. They asked up to play 'Disco Nights.' We played it about six times. After a while, Larkin walked up and said, 'Congratulations, you're an Arista Records artist.'" ● *Disco Nights* (1979) ushered Mr. Q [*right*] and band members Keith Crier (bass), Herb Lane (keyboards), and Paul Service (drums) to platinum status, while the title track topped the R&B chart in April 1979. "Disco Nights (Rock Freak)" was penned from the band's own experience. Mr. Q explains, "We're on stage at these events, performing, looking down at the crowd. You see the people jumping? They don't have a care in the world. Imagine what *we're* feeling. That's 'Disco Nights.' It's that whole experience of recapturing, in our laymen's terms, what we were experiencing—'The feeling's right and the music's tight on the disco night.'" ● Photographed at Osko's Disco in Los Angeles, the album cover offered a thematic gateway to the music. "I think it's what the GQ brand became to people, the fashion," says Mr. Q, attired in a stylish suit for the group's second album *GQ Two* (1980). "It was all things classy, fun, relevant." In style and substance, GQ fully personified their name.

GQ
TWO

ASHFORD & SIMPSON

"It was the age of Studio 54 and this freedom in the clubs," Valerie Simpson recalls about the late-1970s. "We were those people who would wake up at two o'clock in the morning and go to a club." A song that Ashford & Simpson wrote, produced, and/or recorded themselves regularly played at any number of those clubs, especially in the duo's home base of New York. ● Ashford & Simpson's own records were mainstays throughout the decade, including "One More Try," "Over and Over," "Tried, Tested and Found True," "Don't Cost You Nothing," "It Seems to Hang On," and "Bourgie, Bourgie," a sprawling instrumental that was among the records that Larry Levan played during "construction parties" at 84 King Street before the official opening of Paradise Garage in January 1978. Even before they produced "Bourgie, Bourgie" for Gladys Knight & the Pips, Ashford & Simpson recorded a lustrous vocal rendition of the song with John Davis & the Monster Orchestra on *The Monster Strikes Again* (1979). ● As songwriters, Ashford & Simpson penned a major anthem with Chaka Khan's "I'm Every Woman" off her debut album, *Chaka* (1978). "She was such a fireball that she could deliver it and make it believable," says Simpson. "Everybody can't sing that. You have to be able to *be* that. She certainly could handle it. We all felt that way about her." ● A week after the duo's production for *The Boss* (1979) by Diana Ross crowned the disco chart, Ashford & Simpson topped the chart with tracks from their own album, *Stay Free* (1979), including "Found a Cure," "Nobody Knows," and the rousing title track. "Disco was the outlet to stay in the game," says Simpson. "If they're gonna go in another direction, either you get onboard or you say, 'Alright I'll wait till it comes back around to what I'm doing.' We were selling more records and maybe a little freer about taking our chances. We put that beat under there. Let's just make sure that we're *saying* something on top of the beat."

CANDI STATON

"Disco got me out of the chitlin' circuit," says Candi Staton. It was a world apart between Studio 54 and the small clubs Staton performed in during the early-'70s. However, by 1979, Staton had reinvented herself from recording a series of acclaimed albums in Muscle Shoals to becoming a dynamic voice in the clubs. ● Songwriter/producer Dave Crawford, whose production of "Mighty High" for Mighty Clouds of Joy topped the disco chart in 1976, helped steer Staton in a new direction at Warner Bros. "I'm writing a song that's going to last forever," the producer told Staton. And it was Staton's life story that shaped every word of "Young Hearts Run Free." ● "We used to go to lunch together," Staton recalls. "David would write as I spoke about what I was going through with this guy. I think every female artist out here has run into one or two con men. It's hard to get away from a con man! He was threatening me and putting fear in me. David wrote it down. He was writing down things I said. My story was the same as that record. I didn't have to listen to that song but once when I knew that I was singing my story. I did one take on that song. It was like a divine connection. The music was speaking to me. He told me to come back in the studio and listen. I said, 'No, I was just practicing.' He said, 'That was *real*. You can sing it as many times as you want to but I got what I want.'" ● "Young Hearts Run Free" topped the R&B chart and reached the Top 10 on the disco charts in 1976. Staton's popularity in the clubs continued with "Destiny," "Run to Me," a cover of the Bee Gees' "Nights on Broadway," "Victim," and "When You Wake Up Tomorrow," which she produced with Jimmy Simpson on her album *Chance* (1979). With disco as the backdrop, Staton's story was no longer one of heartache... but triumph.

LOLEATTA HOLLOWAY

Record World declared *Loleatta* (1977) "an instant classic." Produced by Norman Harris, the album inaugurated his Gold Mind imprint for Salsoul Records and launched Loleatta Holloway's tenure with the company. Holloway became known for her unscripted asides on songs like "Dreamin'" and "Hit and Run." ● "When they gave me a song, and the song was so long they didn't know what to do in the vamps, they would say, 'Well, let her go herself.'" she explained years later in an interview with British DJ Bill Brewster. "I'd just go straight from the top of my head, whatever I felt in the moment." ● In a field with no shortage of powerhouse vocalists, DJs sensed something distinctive about Holloway [pictured with Frankie Crocker]. "The first time I heard 'Dreamin',' I knew I had never heard anything as special as Loleatta's voice," legendary DJ and producer Jellybean Benitez recalls. "It oozed with passion and intensity." She channeled those qualities into seminal cuts with The Salsoul Orchestra on "Run Away" and "Seconds." "When I first met Loleatta, it was in the recording studio," said Patrick Adams, who produced the latter track. "I was prepared for an encounter with a lioness. True to my expectations, Loleatta roared through the first take. In my lifetime, only a handful of vocalists have given a chilling first-take performance." ● The Chicago-based vocalist's recordings with Dan Hartman only cemented her regard as a vocalist of unparalleled power. Her guest vocals on Hartman's "Vertigo/Relight My Fire" topped the disco chart for six weeks in January of 1980. Just a few months later, Hartman wrote and produced "Love Sensation" for the singer. Tom Moulton's mix of the song gave her another number one disco classic. "It was a big thrill for me to do 'Love Sensation,'" says Moulton. "Loleatta really sang from the bottom of her soul. She *really* felt it. ● "She put the message across, whatever she was doing."

SHALAMAR

"We were all in bloom, so to speak," original Shalamar vocalist Jody Watley says about *Disco Gardens* (1978). It was the second Shalamar album but the first to feature an actual group versus the studio singers that recorded *Uptown Festival* (1977). ● *Soul Train* founder and host Don Cornelius had selected dancers Watley and Jeffrey Daniel [left] to join singer Gary Mumford in promoting the first Shalamar album on Soul Train Records, which eventually folded into Dick Griffey's Solar Records. Soul Train Gang vocalist Gerald Brown replaced Mumford and rounded out the first legitimate lineup of the group, who became one of Solar's signature acts. ● "Gerald helped me personally to be a lot more confident," says Watley. "He'd always say, 'Your tone is everything.' His voice and his presence is very regal." Producer Leon Sylvers shrouded the trio's vocals with an irresistible blend of pop, soul, and disco on songs like "Take That to the Bank" and "Tossing, Turning, and Swinging." ● Howard Hewett [right] replaced Brown and introduced the "classic" Shalamar lineup on *Big Fun* (1979). "Howard's delivery on all the songs we did was fantastic," says Watley. "My background vocals have always been the anchor of the Shalamar sound. As Gerald and Leon Sylvers called it at one point, it's the 'poppiness' that gives it that youthful sound. No matter who's singing lead, that sound is my voice anchoring it." ● A few months after the album's release in 1979, "The Second Time Around" became the trio's biggest pop hit and crowned the R&B chart. "The theme of it is just a feel-good record, which many of our songs were, but that one... I think people really connected to the sentiment of that song," says Watley. "The Second Time Around" also ushered in the new decade: it became the first number one dance hit of the 1980s.

DIANA ROSS

Billboard named Diana Ross "Female Entertainer of the Century" in 1976. That same year, she topped the pop, R&B, and disco charts with "Love Hangover," her first foray into the clubs. It was slinky, sensual, and a completely new sound for the singer. ● Ashford & Simpson refined that sound on Ross's last album of the decade, *The Boss* (1979), contouring each track with a combination of strength and sophistication. From the dramatic opener "No One Gets the Prize" to the low-key grooves of "It's My House," more than half the album was devoted to the dance floor. ● "When we did *The Boss*, Diana was stepping away from Berry Gordy," Valerie Simpson recalls. "She said, 'I want songs that reflect what I'm going through.' It made it very easy to do a song like 'The Boss' because that's what she had become in her own life. She's her own person now. Vocally, we wanted Diana to show off a little more and take more risks. We put her in keys that would stretch her, so she's at the top of her range. She really stepped into her own to sing full-out, full voice. ● "We wrote 'The Boss' as a ballad, but we realized that the ballad didn't do it justice. I decided to invigorate the song by giving it a tempo. It became 'bossier'! The beat made it a more interesting and more fun song. When it gets to that breakdown and she starts whooping, many people thought that was me and it wasn't. We caught Diana in a glorious, free moment. It was totally spontaneous. She felt that." ● "The Boss" powered Diana Ross back to number one on the disco chart and made the singer a dynamic force at Studio 54... on record, on the dance floor, and even in the DJ booth!

REFERENCES

Artists interviewed by Christian John Wikane:

Al McKay—January 22, 2016
Alec R. Costandinos—July 7, 2019
Alfa Anderson—March 28, 2024 & October 19, 2018
Amii Stewart—October 9, 2024
André De Shields—September 23, 2020
Barry Blue—March 17, 2015
Barry Gibb—July 16, 2012
Bernie Worrell—February 21, 2009
Bob Etsy—February 28, 2009
Bobby Eli—December 11, 2012
Bobby Watson—July 2, 2024
Bruce Sudano—February 22, 2010
Candi Staton—November 17, 2024
Cassandra Wooten—August 30, 2013
Cerrone—February 5, 2013
Charles Calello—January 31, 2010
Cheryl Lynn—September 4, 2024
Cheryl Mason-Dorman—August 31, 2013
Chris Amoo—August 28 & 29, 2020
Christian Holder—September 5, 2023
Cory Daye—April 13, 2021
D.C. LaRue—*February 22, 2009*
Debbie Harry—August 22, 2007
Denny Randell—February 1, 2010
Donna Summer—January 15, 2003; February 25, 2009; & June 18, 2011
Earl Young—July 18, 2024
Eddie Irons—August 27, 2024
Eddie Levert—April 6, 2011
Emanuel Rahiem LeBlanc—May 26, 2016
Evelyn "Champagne" King—January 30, 2014
Felipe Rose—December 19, 2019
Fonzi Thornton—October 21, 2020
France Joli—July 31, 2024
George Johnson—November 24, 2010
George McCrae—May 29, 2024
Giorgio Moroder—June 24, 2009
Gloria Gaynor—June 17, 2015
Godfrey Diamond—July 13, 2024
Gwen Dickey—September 28, 2015
Harold Brown—June 11, 2024
Harold Faltermeyer—June 2018, 2020
Henry Stone—December 6, 2012
Ish Ledesma—August 31, 2024
James "Diamond" Williams—October 13, 2017
Janice-Marie Johnson—August 19, 2010
Jody Watley—February 26, 2018
Joe Bataan—July 6, 2024
Joe Esposito—February 20 & September 24, 2010
Kathy Sledge—June 24, 2020 & April 6, 2024
Keith Killgo—June 11, 2024
Keith Wilder—March 20, 2015
Kym Miller—August 9, 2024
Leroy Goméz—May 10, 2009
Linda Clifford—July 11, 2014
Lucy Neale—February 23, 2014
Luther Waters—September 11, 2019
Marc Chantereau—August 14, 2024
Mary Seymour—October 11, 2024
Maurice White—January 7, 2016
Melba Moore—November 29, 2010; January 2015, 2016; & June 25, 2020
Michael Zager—February 15, 2012
Nicky Siano—September 15, 2011
Nile Rodgers—October 3, 2007
Nona Hendryx—April 21, 2013 & March 26, 2015
Norma Jean Wright—September 15, 2024
Oren Waters—September 11, 2019
Patrick Adams—April 30, 2013
Pattie Brooks—March 1, 2020
Pete Belotte—August 30, 2019 & June 17, 2020
Ray Parker, Jr.—October 28, 2022
Raymond Earl—August 9, 2024
Rochelle Fleming—May 4, 2013 & August 16, 2018
Ruth Pointer—July 2, 2020 & May 23, 2022
Sandy Linzer—January 31, 2010
Sarah Dash—May 2, 2013
Sylvester Levay—May 31, 2014
Teri DeSario—September 12, 2024
Thelma Houston—August 16, 2007 & June 29, 2011
Theo Coakley—June 28, 2024
Thom Bell—April 21, 2011; August 18, 2015; & June 22, 2016
Tim Rice—February 13, 2019
Tom Moulton—February 16 & October 25, 2011; June 11 & November 25, 2015
Tomi Jenkins—March 19, 2009
Tony Bongiovi—November 5, 2024
Valerie Holiday—December 8, 2010
Valerie Simpson—December 17, 2015; January 31, 2019; & October 20, 2020
Verdine White—October 14, 2024
Vince Aletti—September 27, 2013
Walter Williams—April 6, 2011
Wanda Vaughn—January 24, 2016
William Anderson—December 4, 2017
Yvonne Elliman—February 22, 2019

Further Reading:

Aletti, Vince (2018) *The Disco Files 1973-1978: New York's Underground, Week by Week*, D.A.P./Distributed Art Publishers, Inc.

Baines, Josh (2016), 'François K Reflects on the Everlasting Legacy of Larry Levan and Paradise Garage', *VICE*, July 14.

Batey, Angus (2012), 'Remembering The Everything Man: A Jimmy Castor Interview', *The Quietus*, January 20.

Beta, Andy (2016), '10 Classic Songs from the Loft, David Mancuso's Influential Dance Party', *Pitchfork*, November 16.

'Billboard 1975 Trendsetter Awards Based on Achievements in 1974' (1974), *Billboard*, Billboard Publications, December 26.

BONEY M INTERVIEWS Bobby Farrell- Marcia Barrett- Liz Mitchell- Maizie Williams, viewed on Freeman Skywatcher YouTube channel (Accessed: January 30, 2025).

Boney M – Story Top Of The Pops with Maizie Williams, viewed on elnoi YouTube channel (Accessed: January 30, 2025).

Bosso, Joe (2014), 'Classic tracks: Harry Wayne Casey on KC And The Sunshine Band's Get Down Tonight', *MusicRadar*, July 15.

Brewster, Bill and Broughton, Frank (2016), 'Interview: David Mancuso', *Red Bull Music Academy*, November 15.

Brewster, Bill (2018), 'Loleatta Holloway: Queen of the Night', *Red Bull Music Academy*, January 22.

Brewster, Bill (2019), 'Steve D'Acquisto, Disco Pioneer', *Red Bull Music Academy*, January 4.

Bronson, Fred (2003) *The Billboard Book of Number 1 Hits*, Billboard Books.

Brown, James and Tucker, Bruce (1986), *James Brown: The Godfather of Soul*, Thunder's Mouth Press.

Carson, Johnny (1974), Jackson 5, *The Tonight Show Starring Johnny Carson*. NBC, November 15.

Cartwright, Garth (2021), 'Our ethos was happy music and good vibes': genre-busting Black British band Osibisa', *The Guardian*, April 29.

'Singles Reviews' (1976), *Cash Box*, The Cash Box Publishing Co. Inc., July 24.

Casas, Àngel (1979), Tina Turner, *Musical Express*. RTVE, May 29.

Cheren, Mel (2000), *Keep on Dancin': My Life and the Paradise Garage*, 24 Hours For Life, Inc.

Christgau, Robert 'Sylvester: Step II' (1978), (Accessed: 30 January 2025).

Clinton, George with Greenman, Ben (2014) *Brothers Be, Yo Like George, Ain't That Funkin' Kinda Hard on You?*, Atria Paperback.

Cobbinah, Angela (2021), 'Teddy Osei: "Happiness was our vibe"', *The Review*, August 19.

Cooper, Kevin (2018), 'INTERVIEW: Ralph Tavares', *UK Music Reviews*, October 21.

Cornelius, Don (1979), McFadden & Whitehead, *Soul Train*. WNEW-TV, November 3.

Costandinos, Alec R. Liner notes to Alec R. Costandinos, *Romeo And Juliet / The Hunchback Of Notre Dame*, Self-released (2011).

Delhaye, Eric (2020), 'Manu Dibango Tells His Life Story', *Medium*, March 24.

Ditlea, Steve (1976), 'Florida Funk—Hot Stuff From Hialeah', *The New York Times*, March 7.

'Doctor's Orders! Studio 54 diva Carol Douglas keeps the disco flame alive' (2013), *The Montreal Gazette*, Postmedia Network, August 30.

Egn, Jack (1978), 'Cashing In on the Boogie to a Tune of $5 Billion', *The Washington Post*, June 25.

Ehrlich, Dimitri (2013), 'New Again: James Brown', *Interview*, October 23.

Emerson, Ken (1979), 'Disco Is Not Just for Dancing', *The New York Times*, April 22.

'Errol Brown: Singer and songwriter whose band Hot Chocolate had a string of infectious hits but also dealt with serious subjects' (2015), *The Independent*, May 9.

Ford Jr., Robert (1979), 'Panel Traces Evolution of Pop-Disco', *Billboard*, March 24.

Fowden, Barry (2000), 'Talking with Dennis Edwards', *Soul Cellar*, July 5.

Freeland, Nat (1973), 'Col/Philly Cooperation Bolsters Blue Notes' Hit', *Billboard*, December 22.

Goldstein, Patrick (1979), '"CUBA." The Gibson Brothers', *The Los Angeles Times*, December 23.

Grein, Paul (1979), 'Memphis Teacher's Disk Cracks Top 10', *Billboard*, June 9.

'Hancock to Ignore Disco Drift Critics' (1979), *Billboard*, Billboard Publications, February 3.

Hankin, Noel (2021), 'After Dark: Birth of the Disco Dance Party', Leon Niknah Publishing Company.

Hannigan, Ingrid (1973), ''Soul Makossa' hit Slowed by Covers', *Billboard*, June 30.

Harrison, Ed (1976), 'Crossovers Vibist Ayers' Aim', *Billboard*, December 25.

Holden, Stephen (2000), 'Vicki Sue Robinson, 46, Singer of Disco Anthem', *The New York Times*, May 2.

'Interview: Manu Dibango' (1991), *UNESCO Courier*, United Nations Educational, Scientific and Cultural Organization (UNESCO), May.

'Interview—William King of Commodores' (2019), *Cryptic Rock* magazine, Cryptic Rock, July 5.

Isaac Hayes: A Conversation (2005), Georgia Public Broadcasting (GPB), viewed on GPB YouTube channel (Accessed: January 30, 2025).

'Isaac Hayes: Don't Let Go' (1979), *Billboard*, Billboard Publications, September 8.

Jacobson, Mark (1974) 'Hollyw-o-o-o-d! The Return of the New York Disco', *New York* magazine, July 1.

Jefferson, Shelley Nicole. Liner notes to Kool & the Gang, *Open Sesame* [Expanded Edition], CDBBR0045 (2011).

Jonze, Tim (2014), 'Abba on drugs, Eminem and why writing great pop is a job for young people', *The Guardian*, April 10.

Kurtz, Warren (2019), 'Fabulous Flip Sides—Interview with Anita Ward', *Goldmine*, December 8.

'Labels Mix Records for Club Scene' (1974), *Billboard*, Billboard Publications, November 2.

Langmead, Jon (2015), 'Heavy Hitters: An Interview with The Isley Brothers', *PopMatters*, August 4.

Lawrence, Tim (2004) *Love Saves the Day: A History of American Dance Music Culture, 1970-1979*, Duke University Press Books.

Maslin, Janet (1979), 'Why the Bee Gees Sound So Good', *The New York Times*, February 18.

'McCoy Honored' (1976), *Record World*, Record World Publishing Co. Inc., June 12

McGeoch, Callum (2014), 'Sylvia Robinson: rapper's delight', *Dazed*, October 19.

Melchior, Al (2024), 'Who Did It Best? 4 Versions of Eddie Floyd and Steve Cropper's "Knock on Wood"', *American Songwriter*, February 14.

Moulton, Tom (1975), 'Disco Action', *Billboard*, February 22.

'New on the Charts' (1974), *Billboard*, Billboard Publications, December 7.

O'Brien, Phil (2021), 'Religion, Disco, Death and Drama—Westside Theatre's History Reads Like a Play in 3 Acts', *W42ST*, September 21.

Orlov, Piotr (2020), *Still Saving the Day: The Most Influential Dance Party in History*, NPR, February 19.

Orth, Maureen (1979), 'The Beat Comes East: New York's Record Biz goes Solid Gold', *New York* magazine, March 26.

Palm, Carl Magnus. Liner notes to ABBA, *Voulez-Vous* [Deluxe Edition], B003IB38UM, (2010).

Pantella, Marco (2014), 'An Interview with Amanda Lear', *The GROUND* magazine, March 10.

Paoletta, Michael (1999), 'Vicki Sue Robinson Comes Back Around', *Billboard*, May 1.

Parker, Lyndsey (2023), 'Keith Richards, Mick Jagger talk 'Some Girls' anniversary: Punk rock was "a kick up our a**"', *Yahoo Entertainment*, June 8.

Parker, Marc and Parker, Melissa Benefield, 'Thomas McClary Interview: Commodores Co-Founder Talks Lionel Richie and Famed Group's Beginnings', *Smashing Interviews*, September 29.

Partridge, Rob (1972), 'Black Music on Its Own in U.K.', *Billboard*, December 2.

Philadelphia: The Great Experiment (2013), Directed by Andrew Ferrett and Sam Katz, US: History Making Productions.

Poet, J. (2014), 'Harry Wayne Casey: The Boogie Man Returns', GRAMMY.com, December 3.

Quindlen, Anna (1977), 'What's New in the Discotheques', *The New York Times*, November 11.

Radcliffe, Joe (1976), 'Disco Music Sounds Undergoing Changes', *Billboard*, October 2.

Radcliffe, Joe (1977), 'McCoy Striving to Blast Image as "Disco Kid"', *Billboard*, December 10.

'RCA Pushing Plugs for Main Ingredient' (1974), *Billboard*, Billboard Publications, August 3.

Richards, Sam (2016), '"He was like the Messiah": Larry Levan, the DJ who changed dance music forever', *The Guardian*, March 28.

Robinson, Leroy (1973), 'Kendricks Truckin' On Way to Top', *Billboard*, November 3.

Robinson, Leroy (1974), 'RCA's Team Won't Quit; Cite "Boat"', Billboard, November 9.

Rockwell, John (1978), 'The Bee Gees Are Getting as Big As the Beatles', *The New York Times*, March 19.

Rockwell, John (1979), 'Can Rock and Disco Music Coexist?', *The New York Times*, January 21.

Rockwell, John (1979), 'The Pop Life', *The New York Times*, July 13.

Roy Ayers Interview (2016), viewed on MRW Directs YouTube channel, (Accessed: January 30, 2025).

Schaffer, Noah (2018), 'Music Interview: Ernie Isley Keeps R&B Guitar Alive', The Arts Fuse, January 16.

Schoenberger, Francis (2019), 'He Said, She Said: An Interview with John Lennon', SPIN, October 9.

Sexton, Paul (2024), 'Cloud Nine': The Story Behind The Temptations' High-Flying Hit,' udiscovermusic.com, October 25.

Slotnik, Daniel E. (2020), 'Hamilton Bohannon, Driving Disco Drummer, Dies at 78', *The New York Times*, May 2.

Soul Man: Isaac Hayes (2003), Directed by Steve Condie and Nick Copus, US: BBC.

Stanley, Bob (2023), 'The feelin' was right: how the Bee Gees ruled late 70s pop', *The Guardian*, June 2.

Stephenson, Will (2017), 'Suite for Bohannon', *Oxford American*, July 27.

Stewart, Rod (2012) *Rod: The Autobiography*, Three Rivers Press.

Stone, Sly with Greenman, Ben (2023), *Thank You (Falettinme Be Mice Elf Again): A Memoir*, Auwa Books.

Super B-Beat Show (2010), *Jimmy Castor interview on The Super B-Beat Show 1/31/2010* [Podcast], accessed on YouTube (January 30, 2025).

'Talent in Action Showcases Top Awards Winners' (1973), *Billboard*, Billboard Publications, December 29.

Tavares - TopPop Interview (Raw material) 02-01-1978 (1978), viewed on TopPop YouTube channel, (Accessed: January 30, 2025).

The best-selling singles of all time on the Official UK Chart (2023), (Accessed: 30 January 2025).

The Disco Scene of 1976 (1976), Maryland Public Broadcasting, viewed on dirtydiscosecrets YouTube channel, (Accessed: 30 January 2025).

The International Disco Sourcebook (1977), 'The world's only Directory exclusively for the Disco Industry' [Advert] *Billboard*, 26 February 1977, p. 69.

'The Main Ingredient: Happiness Is Just Around the Bend' (1974), *Billboard*, Billboard Publications, June 8.

'The Salsoul Orchestra Keeps Disco Dancing' (1976), *Billboard*, Billboard Publications, October 16.

Thomas, Andy (2020), 'Bounce, Rock, Skate, Roll', *WaxPoetics*, December 9.

'Top Single Picks' (1974), *Billboard*, Billboard Publications, October 19.

'Top Single Picks' (1978), *Billboard*, Billboard Publications, January 21.

'Trammps Cart Away 3 Major Accolades' (1976), *Billboard*, Billboard Publications, October 9.

'Van McCoy, Composed "The Hustle," Hit in '75' (1979), *The New York Times*, July 7.

VH1 Presents the '70s: Disco Explosion (1996), VH1 August 23.

Warhol, Andy (1975), 'A Taste of Paradis: Diana Ross, in Conversation With Andy Warhol', *Interview Magazine*, September.

Waring, Charles (2012) 'Still on the Wright Path—Veteran Soul Diva Betty Wright Speaks to SJF', *Soul&Jazz&Funk*, July 23.

Wikane, Christian John (2019), 'Mahalo, Mary Magdalene: An Interview with Chart-Topping GRAMMY Winner Yvonne Elliman', *PopMatters*, March 4.

Wikane, Christian John (2021), ''Cherchez La Femme' at 45: An Interview with GRAMMY-nominated Vocalist Cory Daye', *PopMatters*, May 28.

Wikane, Christian John, Liner notes to Bonnie Pointer, *Bonnie Pointer* [Expanded Edition], CDBBR0093 (2012).

Wikane, Christian John, Liner notes to Loleatta Holloway, *Dreamin' The Loleatta Holloway Anthology 1976-1982*, CDBBRD0181 (2014).

Wikane, Christian John, Liner notes to Michael Zager Band, *Let's All Chant* [Expanded Edition], CRPOP99 (2012).

Wolfe, Linda (1972), 'The Animal Fare', *New York* magazine, May 29.

Wolk, Douglas (2012) 'Kindness' Album Title Hints at the Origin of Disco', *MTV.com*, May 9.

Wyman, Bill (1990), *Stone Alone*, Viking.

Picture Credits

Page	Credit
Endpapers, front	*Michael Ochs Archives/Getty Images*
Endpapers, back	*Harry Langdon/Archive Photos/Getty Images*
2	*Ralph Dominguez / Media Punch / Alamy Stock Photo*
6	*Michael Ochs Archives/Getty Images*
9	*Alan Tannenbaum/Getty Images*
15	*David Redfern/Redferns/Getty Images*
17	*Rolls Press/Popperfoto/Getty Images*
19	*David Farrell/Redferns/Getty Images*
21	*Michael Ochs Archives/Getty Images*
23	*David Redfern/Redferns/Getty Images*
25	*-/AFP/Getty Images*
27	*TPLP/Archive Photos/Getty Images*
29	*Don Hunstein © Sony Music Entertainment*
31	*Michael Ochs Archives/Getty Images*
33	*Sherry Rayn Barnett/Michael Ochs Archives/Getty Images*
35 (& endpapers, front)	*Jim Britt/Michael Ochs Archive/Getty Images*
37	*K.Abe/Getty Images*
39	*Michael Ochs Archives/Getty Images*
41	*Michael Ochs Archives/Getty Images*
47	*Laurent MAOUS/Gamma-Rapho/Getty Images*
49	*Tim Graham/Hulton Archive/Getty Images*
51	*Soul Train/Getty Images*
53	*Michael Ochs Archives/Getty Images*
55	*Michael Ochs Archives/Getty Images*
57	*Michael Ochs Archives/Getty Images*
59	*The Estate of David Gahr/Premium Archive/Getty Images*
61	*Photo by GAB Archive/Redferns via Getty Images*
63	*David Redfern/Redferns/Getty Images*
65	*Photo by GAB Archive/Redferns via Getty Images*
67	*Michael Ochs Archives/Getty Images*
69	*Michael Ochs Archives/Getty Images*
71	*Fin Costello/Redferns/Getty Images*
73	*Michael Ochs Archives/Getty Images*
75	*Michael Ochs Archives/Getty Images*
77	*Michael Ochs Archives/Getty Images*
79	*Angelo Deligio/Mondadori Portfolio/Getty Images*
81	*ChrisWalterPhotography.com*
83	*Michael Ochs Archives/Getty Images*
85	*Michael Ochs Archives/Getty Images*
87	*CBS/Getty Images*
89	*Mirrorpix/Getty Images*
91	*Soul Train/Getty Images*
93	*Gems/Redferns/Getty Images*
95	*Helmut Reiss/United Archives/Hulton Archive/Getty Images*
96–97	*John Barrett/PHOTOlink/Alamy Stock Photo*
103	*David Gahr/Premium Archive/Getty Images*
105	*Michael Ochs Archives/Getty Images*
107	*Michael Ochs Archives/Getty Images*
109	*Michael Ochs Archives/Getty Images*
111	*PL Gould/Images Press/Archive Images/Getty Images*
113	*Michael Ochs Archives/Getty Images*
115	*Michael Ochs Archives/Getty Images*
117	*Michael Ochs Archives/Getty Images*
119	*Courtesy of Cory Dave*
121	*Allan Tannenbaum/Getty Images*
123	*Gilles Petard/Redferns/Getty Images*
125	*United Archives/Hulton Archive/Getty Images*
127	*Don Hunstein © Sony Music Entertainment*
129	*Rick Diamond/Archive Photos/Getty Images*
131	*Michael Ochs Archives/Getty Images*
133	*Paul Slade/Paris Match/Getty Images*
135	*Michael Ochs Archives/Getty Images*
137	*Echoes/Redferns/Getty Images*
139	*Echoes/Redferns/Getty Images*
141	*Sonia Moskowitz/Archive Photos/Getty Images*
143	*Richard E. Aaron/Redferns/Getty Images*
145	*Michael Ochs Archives/Getty Images*
147	*Courtesy of D.C. LaRue*
149	*David Redfern/Redferns/Getty Images*
151	*ChrisWalterPhotography.com*
153	*Afro Newspaper/Gado/Archive Images/Getty Images*
155	*Photo by GAB Archive/Redferns via Getty Images*
157	*Steve Schapiro/Corbis/Getty Images*
159	*LGI Stock/Corbis/VCG/Getty Images*
161	*Michael Ochs Archives/Getty Images*
163	*Michael Ochs Archives/Getty Images*
169	*Jean-Louis Atlan/Sygma/Getty Images*
171	*Michael Putland/Hulton Archive/Getty Images*
173	*Echoes/Redferns/Getty Images*
175	*Reporters Associati & Archivi/Mondadori Portfolio Premium/Getty Images*
177	*Pictorial Press / Alamy Stock Photo*
179	*Ebet Roberts*
181	*Bettman/Getty Images*
183	*Michael Ochs Archives/Getty Images*
185	*Chuck Fishman/Premium Archive/Getty Images*
187	*Courtesy of Norma Jean Wright*
189	*Photo by GAB Archive/Redferns via Getty Images*
191	*Mirrorpix/Getty Images*
193	*Gilles Petard/Redferns/Getty Images*
195	*Michael Putland/Premium Archive/Getty Images*
197	*Don Hunstein © Sony Music Entertainment*
199	*James Kriegsmann/Michael Ochs Archives/Getty Images*
201	*Photo by GAB Archive/Redferns via Getty Images*
203	*Jacques Aubert / Universal Music France / Bridgeman Images*
205	*Harry Langdon/Archive Photos/Getty Images*
207	*ChrisWalterPhotography.com*
209	*Paul Natkin/Archive Photos/Getty Images*
211	*Records/Alamy*
213	*Steve Wood/Popperfoto/Getty Images*
215	*Soul Train/Getty Images*
217	*Ralph Dominguez / Media Punch / Alamy Stock Photo*
219	*Lynn Goldsmith/Corbis Historical/VCG/Getty Images*
221	*Roberta Bayley/Redferns/Getty Images*
223 (& endpapers, back)	*Richard E. Aaron/Redferns/Getty Images*
225	*Courtesy of Len Kaltman*
227	*Michael Ochs Archives/Getty Images*
229	*Harry Langdon/Archive Photos/Getty Images*
231	*Sobli/RDB/Ullstein Bild Dtl/Ullstein Bild/Getty Images*
233	*Michael Ochs Archives/Echoes/Redferns/Getty Images*
235	*Harry Langdon/Archive Photos/Getty Images*
237	*Paul Natkin/Archive Photos/Getty Images*
239	*Lynn McAfee / Performing Arts Images / Alamy Stock Photo*
241	*Courtesy of Sony Music Entertainment*
243	*Afro American Newspapers/Gado/Archive Photos/Getty Images*
245	*Echoes/Redferns/Getty Images*
247	*Fran Pelzman/Ebet Roberts Studio/Redferns/Getty Images*
249	*Michael Ochs Archives/Getty Images*
251	*Richard Corkery/NY Daily News Archive/Getty Images*

ACKNOWLEDGMENTS

This book is dedicated with love to my greatest supporter, Stanley!

With love to my amazing and beautiful children; Ben, Jessie, Samantha and David, and triple my blessings for Noah, Elizabeth and Emmy! And thank you to my family and my friends!

To Christian John Wikane, my collaborator, my partner in shared ideas, and most of all my very dearest friend, thank you and love you. Thanks to our bestie, Donna Summer!

To James Smith, thank you for your continuing encouragement, inspiration, vision, and wisdom. I am grateful.

To our fabulous team at ACC Art Books: John Brancati, Andrew Whittaker, Stewart Norvill, Carol Leggett, Steven Farrow, Mariona Vilarós Capella, and Corban Wilkin; thank you for your patience and support!

Alice Harris

Thank you to my sister Amy, for sharing her record collection with me; my Aunt Gail for bringing Casablanca Records into my life; and my parents, whose love of music lives within me.

My friends and colleagues, your support has made a tremendous difference in my life. Thank you, Nona Hendryx and Vicki Wickham, for your belief in me, from the very beginning.

Sekou Luke, my "Unscripted" production partner, for sharing the vision and passion to document the stories of legendary artists who've kept us dancing and dreaming.

To all of the artists, songwriters, and producers I've had the honor of interviewing over the past 25 years, thank you for a lifetime of inspiration. And thank you Valerie Simpson for composing the majestic "Ain't No Mountain High Enough"—it's the reason I write about music.

Thank you to Verdine White of Earth, Wind & Fire, for writing the foreword and for so many wonderful conversations over the years. You ARE a "Shining Star"!

My DJ friends in NYC, for creating unforgettable nights on the dance floor throughout the course of writing this book: Qool DJ Marv, DJ Spinna, DJ Lina, Emil Cohen / Motherdisco, Bill Coleman, Greg Caz, Frankie Paradise, and the Vinyl Nights crew.

John Brancati, Andrew Whittaker, Stewart Norvill, Steven Farrow, Carol Leggett, and everyone at ACC Art Books... thank you for joining us at the disco! James Smith, CEO of ACC Art Books, thank you for all of your creativity and kindness, and for exemplifying what it means to be a leader.

Alice Harris, I am forever grateful that Donna Summer brought us together in 2008. We've shared so much joy and laughter over the years. Thank you for your friendship, your impeccable style, and for being the spark behind our literary adventures. You are a rare treasure. I'm ready for the next dance!

Christian John Wikane

Additional thanks to those who helped coordinate artist interviews and secure photos: Amir Bayyan, Cleveland Uhuru-Sasa Brown, Bill Carpenter, Barry Collings, Cory Daye, Tracy DiMambro, Lloyd Bolton, Amanda Beel, Roger Heijster, Thurlene Johnson, D.C. LaRue, Len Kaltman, Robert King, Martha Moore, Gail Parenteau, Ebet Roberts, Jon Roberts, Paul Robinson, Jennifer Sakuma, Katie Sheppard, Seth Shomes, Toby Silver, Daniel Vaillancourt, Norma Jean Wright, and Sylvia Young.

p.2 Donna Summer and Michael Jackson at the American Music Awards, 1980.

p.6 Earth, Wind & Fire during an album cover shoot, 1974.

p.9 Studio 54 partygoers dance amid the laser towers
that descended from the ceiling, 1978.

p.96–97 The rush to get into Studio 54, 1978.

The front endpapers feature Marvin Gaye and Diana Ross.
The back endpapers feature George Clinton and Cher.

ISBN: 978 1 78884 279 2

A CIP catalogue record for this book is available from the British Library

The authors and publisher gratefully acknowledge the permission granted to reproduce the copyright material in this book. Every effort has been made to trace copyright holders and to obtain their permission for the use of copyright material. The publisher apologises for any errors or omissions in the text and would be grateful if notified of any corrections that should be incorporated in future reprints or editions of this book.

Text & image research: Christian John Wikane
Editor: Stewart Norvill
Designers: Steve Farrow & Mariona Vilarós Capella
Reprographics Manager: Corban Wilkin

EU GPSR Authorised Representative:
Easy Access System Europe Oü, 16879218
Address: Mustamäe tee 50, 10621 Tallinn, Estonia
Email: gpsr@easproject.com Tel: +358 40 500 3575

Printed in China by C&C Offset Printing Co. Ltd
for ACC Art Books Ltd, Woodbridge, Suffolk, UK

www.accartbooks.com